The Hashemites

Makers
of the
Modern
World

The Hashemites
The Dream of Arabia
Robert McNamara

HH
HAUS HISTORIES

First published in Great Britain in 2009 by
Haus Publishing Ltd
70 Cadogan Place
London SW1X 9AH
www.hauspublishing.com

A CIP catalogue record for this book
is available from the British Library

ISBN 978-1-905791-66-8

Series design by Susan Buchanan
Typeset in Sabon by MacGuru Ltd
Printed in Dubai by Oriental Press
Maps by Martin Lubikowski, ML Design, London

Contents

Preface

There are two striking images of Emir Feisal at the Paris Peace Conference. In William Orpen's famous group portrait *A Peace Conference at the Quai d'Orsay*, standing third from the left, his headdress and desert clothing make a striking contrast with the western suits and uniforms of the other assembled delegates. The other famous picture is of Feisal standing in front of the delegation of the Hejaz. His face looks drawn and full of melancholy, as though he realises the arduous, if not impossible mission, he has been tasked with in Paris. For Feisal, while he sits as the representative of the small desert state of the Hejaz, is also the representative of Arab nationalist aspirations. Furthermore, he is the representative of his father, King Hussein, the former Sherif of Mecca, and his ambitions. In 1916, he has proclaimed himself King of the Arabs. This title remains unrecognised; the British and French view Hussein merely as King of the Hejaz.

It is odd that Hussein chose to send Feisal rather than go to Paris himself. The likeliest reasons are that Hussein is now in his late sixties and he is already having trouble maintaining control of the Hejaz from rivals such as Ibn Saud in the Arabian Peninsula. More importantly, Hussein, perhaps due to age, perhaps due to indolence, had let the military leadership of the Arab Revolt pass into the hands of his most dynamic son, Feisal, who ironically was the most sceptical about the whole enterprise of taking arms against the Turks. It is also fairly clear that the British, especially the influential liaison officer, Thomas Edward (T.E.) Lawrence had little confidence in Hussein's abilities and disliked his apparently inexhaustible capacity for obtuseness and duplicity.

Feisal looks older in these pictures than his thirty-two years. While much of his childhood had been spent in the urban and cosmopolitan setting of turn of the century Constantinople, he had since 1909 lived in the Hejaz. His father encouraged his children to live the frugal and tough lives of the Bedouin when they returned to the Hejaz. The hard fighting of the Arab Revolt also took its inevitable toll. Feisal was a man of action – in constant motion. William Orpen recalls his trouble painting Feisal's portrait because he would get up constantly to see what the artist was painting.[1] He also, like many Arabs of this time, smoked innumerable cigarettes, while tending to eat little food. Indeed he disliked formal European dinners, preferring to get back to drinking coffee and smoking cigarettes; a diet that probably contributed to his early death at 47 in 1933.[2] At the time of the Peace Conference, Feisal played up his Arab credentials and eschewed European dress. Stephen Bonsal, the American diplomat and journalist, recalls the Emir's quarters in a small private hotel in Paris as: 'transformed into something like a nomad's tent…There, with his rakish turban, his gallant gold-embroidered coat, his very visible scimitar, and his bejeweled revolver (by no means concealed), he looks what he doubtless is, a son of Mars, Oriental version.'[3] (Later as King of Iraq, Feisal would reject traditional dress and wear expensive tailored suits to demonstrate his modernity.)

Prior to his departure to Europe, Feisal confided to the British Commander-in-Chief in the Middle East, General Allenby that he was *nervous about the peace settlement.* Allenby reassured him that 'he must trust the Entente powers to treat him fairly.'[4] Feisal had plenty of grounds for doubting the Entente's promises. He was aware of the many contradictory promises that had been made during the War by the British. Some, such as the correspondence between his father and the British High Commissioner in Egypt, seemed to promise independence to the Arab Middle East but were these pledges not trumped by the Sykes-Picot Agreement, which spoke of French and British annexations and spheres of influence in the region? He was also probably aware that the British government viewed the Hashemites' role at the Peace Conference as more than representing the Arab cause. They were also seen as useful tools to prise the French out of key territories in the Middle East that the British coveted. Aligning Britain with Arab nationalism in the new era of self-determination proclaimed by the United States of America's President, Woodrow Wilson, provided an opportunity to further strengthen British power in the Middle East. Any independent Arab state that would emerge from the Peace Conference would almost certainly be subject to British influence and tutelage for many years. It would be far more manageable than dealing with the French. Indeed, French hostility to Arab nationalism might poison British relations with the Arabs as well. Feisal was surely aware of this strategy and probably believed it was the only chance he had of success at the Conference.

The French saw through the British strategy at an early stage. They poured poison about Feisal in the ear of anyone who would listen. They claimed he was an adventurer who counted for nothing in the Arab world and 'was in the pay of English landgrabbers who have formed companies, later to be chartered, which will, under the guise of religion, take over the Arab lands and suck them dry as they have the rest of the world.'[5]

In the photo of the delegation from the Hejaz the other outstanding figure apart from Feisal is the diminutive figure of T E Lawrence. Lawrence is perhaps the most influential figure in Feisal's life. He is responsible for identifying Feisal as the figure to drive the Arab Revolt forward as it stagnated in the months after its outbreak in June 1916. He is the figure who persuades Feisal to follow a strategy of breaking out of the Hejaz and heading north into Syria. This strategy ensures that the Arab irregular forces advance in step with the British forces as they push towards Damascus in 1918. Lawrence orchestrates the liberation of Damascus by Feisal's irregulars rather than British Imperial forces helping guarantee that the voice of the Arabs is heard at the Peace Conference and frustrating French hopes of occupying the city. In November 1918, Lawrence convinced the British government that Feisal was the best figure to represent Arab interests in Paris. As he informed King Hussein on 8 November 1918, 'I hope you will send Feisal since his splendid victories have given him a personal reputation in Europe which will make his success easier'.[6] This decision was to lead to a serious breach between Feisal and Hussein. Hussein felt that Feisal usurped his authority and claims in favour of his own personal aggrandisement. There seems little doubt that Feisal by the time of the Peace Conference was already beginning to be exasperated by his father's intransigence and unrealistic assessment of his true power and influence. This was partly due to Lawrence, who acted as Feisal's political adviser and confidante throughout the Conference. All in all, few dele-gates at the Peace Conference had as difficult a task as Feisal, facing opposition and intrigue from the French and his father. Feisal's hopes, Arab nationalist dreams and Hashemite ambi-tions rested on two shaky pillars. One was that Britain would risk its alliance with France to support Arab aims because it chimed with its own ideas for the Middle East. The other was that President Wilson's doctrine of national self-determina-tion would extend beyond Europe to the Middle East.

Introduction

Peacemaking in the Middle East – The Hashemites: Victors or Victims?

This book is about the making of peace in the Middle East after the First World War. Its focus is on the relationship between the Hashemites, who became the leaders of Arab nationalism almost by accident, and the Allied Powers. It is a story of alleged betrayal of promises, greed, failure and extraordinary reversals of fortune for the leader of the Hashemites, Sherif Hussein, the Emir of Mecca, and his family. By 1922, as a result of the Peace Settlement, one of his sons, Feisal was the King of the new country of Iraq and another Abdullah was Emir of Transjordan. Hussein himself was the King of the Hejaz (what is now part of the north-west of Saudi Arabia). Iraq and Transjordan were Mandates, not independent states, and British advisers wielded influence and power over them. Nonetheless, the sons of a relatively minor Arab potentate ruled two countries, many times the size of Britain, which were guaranteed eventual independence. Indeed, Iraq had to wait only until 1932 to achieve this.

So the story of the Hashemites, one would imagine, should

be written as one of triumph. This is not what happened. Partly, this was due to Hussein's own fate. His Kingdom of Hejaz, which he rightly feared could not survive unless part of a wider Arab entity, was wiped from the map by his foe for supremacy in the Arabian Peninsula, 'Abd al-'Aziz Ibn Saud in 1924–5. He spent the rest of his life in bitter exile in Cyprus, as far from leadership of the Arab world as one can imagine. Aided by the extremely able advocacy of the former colonial administrator George Antonius, Hussein's grievances echoed from beyond the grave. In Antonius' key work, *The Arab Awakening* (1938), a different narrative, not of triumph, but of betrayal and the denial of Arab and Hashemite rights, emerged. Hussein, as Antonius described, believed that the Allies did not deliver what he had been promised during the War in return for his leading the Arab Revolt against the Turks: namely Hashemite leadership of a vast Arab Kingdom encompassing the modern states of Iraq, Syria, Palestine and Jordan, as well as the Hejaz. Hussein's claims of betrayal turn on correspondence he engaged in with the British government's High Commissioner in Egypt, Sir Henry McMahon, during 1915 and 1916. Certainly there are apparent incompatibilities and discrepancies between the promises and understandings given by McMahon to Hussein in this correspondence when one compares them to the secret Sykes-Picot Agreement between the British and French, the Balfour Declaration of 1917 and the eventual peace settlement in the Middle East. The consensus of historical opinion now regards the Hashemite claims with rather a jaundiced eye and views the incompatibilities as more minor than Antonius supposed, though significant debates continue about the question of Palestine. However, Arab political and popular opinion since the First World War does not accept this consensus. Even bitter political foes of the Hashemites, such as President Nasser of Egypt, subscribed enthusiastically to the notion of Allied, particularly British, betrayal of the Arab cause after the First World War.

The long process of peacemaking

The process of making peace after the First World War, the ending of the fighting, the delineation of frontiers and the establishment of stable regimes took longer in the Middle East than virtually anywhere else. The armistice at Mudros in October 1918, which concluded hostilities between the Allied Powers and the Ottomans, was merely a pause in conflict in the Middle East. Inter-Arab conflict for supremacy in the Arabian Peninsula continued between King Hussein of the Hejaz and Ibn Saud, the Emir of Nejd. In Egypt, there was a serious uprising against British rule in 1919. When the San Remo conference of April 1920 announced the allocation of Middle Eastern Mandates to Britain and France, it became clear that the rhetoric of self-determination that the Allies espoused, particularly after the American entry into the War, was, in the main, hollow. As a consequence, a wave of violence spread across Iraq and Syria that was only put down by the massive application of force by Britain and France respectively. In Syria, Feisal's independent Arab Kingdom, which had enjoyed quasi-independence since October 1918 was crushed and Feisal forced into exile.

While all other peace treaties were completed by mid-1920, the fate of the Ottoman territories took much longer to resolve. The Treaty of Sèvres failed when the Turkish nationalist leader Mustafa Kemal defied its provisions and forced the Allies to renegotiate. In the Arab parts of the Middle East, the British and French relied on a number of strategies to enforce their Mandates. France relied on military power and a 'divide and conquer' strategy that emphasised ethnic, religious and tribal differences in its Syrian and Lebanese Mandates. Nonetheless, frequent rebellions and protests marred the quarter-century of French rule in the Levant. Britain at least partially resolved its Middle Eastern conundrum by using the 'Sherifian Solution'. This, agreed in March 1921 at the Cairo Conference of senior British ministers and officials, put in place Arab rulers from the Hashemite family in Iraq and Transjordan. The aim was to allow Britain to maintain its influence and power in these countries by proxy and on the cheap. It was a qualified success that allowed Britain to maintain an influential role in both countries until the late 1950s. In contrast, French political, as opposed to cultural, influence in Syria and Lebanon faded very quickly after independence in 1945. However, the association of the Hashemites with the British arguably damned them as British puppets, particularly in the eyes of post-war Arab nationalists. Even the establishment of relatively stable governments in the region under British and French tutelage was not the end of peacemaking. A revived Turkey under Mustafa Kemal did not finally renounce its claims to the region around the Iraqi city of Mosul until 1925. As late as 1939, the peace settlement in the Middle East could be revisited, when France handed back the Alexandretta region from Syria to Turkey to buy its neutrality during the Second World War.

While the peace process can therefore be traced right up the eve of the Second World War, the end of 1922 saw at least a modicum of stability arrive in the Middle East. The tardiness in making peace appears curious when one considers that the Middle East had received much attention during the War by British and French policymakers. Promises were made to Arabs, to Jews and, of course, to each other regarding the division of territory. Indeed, this was the nub of the problem. So many promises and agreements were made that the Peace Conference found it hard to arbitrate between the various claims brought forward. Britain and France had their own agendas. A weak Arab Kingdom, subject to British guidance, was seen as a means of forestalling French ambitions in the region and protecting British strategic interests. Therefore, Britain was anxious to support Hashemite claims in areas that the French saw as forming part of their own sphere of influence. The United States, for a time, seemed interested in encouraging self-determination in the Middle East. However, the growing wave of isolationism that swept America in 1919 doomed any Arab and Hashemites hopes for support from that quarter. The French, their policy driven by the strong colonial lobby, were determined to assert their rights in the Middle East. The peacemakers concentrated more on the demands of the Great Powers than on the aspirations of the Hashemites and the Arabs. However, the need to appease the Arabs would arise again as it became clear that European rule in the Middle East was impossible without at least their acquiescence.

Hashemite King Hussein ibn 'Ali, Caliph al-Islam, King of the Hejaz,
Commander of the Faithful, Grand Sherif and Emir of Mecca in the early 1920s.
King Hussein proclaimed the independence of all Arabs from the Ottoman
Empire in the Arab Revolt in 1916.

I
The Lives and the Land

1
The Arab World and the Hashemites before the First World War

Ottomans and Arabs

By the outbreak of the First World War, the Turks, who origi-
nated from the Central Asian steppes, had ruled the heart-
lands of the Arab World encompassing the modern-day states
of Syria, Iraq, Jordan, Israel, Saudi Arabia and Arab North
Africa for over a thousand years. Syria, Iraq, Jordan and Palestine were known as the Fertile Crescent due to the important rivers, the Jordan, Tigris and Euphrates, that provided
the water resources that made the areas conducive to human
settlement. However, by 1914, the Arab lands of the Fertile
Crescent and the Arabian Peninsula, the cradle of one of
the world's great civilisations and an all-conquering Islamic
empire, were reduced to little more than barren, poverty-
stricken, disease-ridden and ill-educated backwaters. The
Ottomans, the last of the great Islamic Turkish tribes to forge
a major empire, conquered the Arab lands in 1517 and ruled
them, without serious opposition, for just over four centuries.
Only in the last decades of Ottoman rule did proto-national-
ist challenges begin to emerge in the Arab territories.

When it emerged in the 7th century, Islam was initially synonymous with being Arab. However, within a century of the Arab conquests, religion rather than ethnicity or nationality became 'the Supreme bond'[1] and partly accounts for the willingness of the Arabs to accept Muslim Turkish overlords. Another was the nature of Ottoman rule. While ostensibly one of the most centralised empires in the world with all power held by the Sultan, this was, as one observer noted, 'make-believe'.[2] Outside the main urban centres, such as Damascus, Aleppo, Mosul and Baghdad, government control was weak and the Arabic-speaking societies of the Fertile Crescent were split into groupings based on family, tribal, ethnic and religious ties.[3]

While Turkish-speaking governors, in theory, held supreme power in the Arabic-speaking regions, in practice linguistic barriers and a lack of military power meant they were dependent on local tribal leaders, the urban rich and religious leaders to maintain even a modicum of influence. These leading groups were known as the 'Notables'. The politics of these Notables was the dominant fact of political life in the Ottoman Middle East in the 19th and early 20th century.[4]

The French Revolution and the growth of concepts such as nationalism and patriotism in the early 19th century intrigued Ottoman and Muslim thinkers. While the Ottomans and Muslim culture generally had viewed the infidels of Europe with repugnance, no one could but fail to be impressed by the patriotic zeal of the French Revolutionary armies. Moreover, the gradual integration of the Ottoman Empire into the periphery of the developing world capitalist economy of the early and mid-19th century spurred on the copying of Western ideas and technology. The Ottoman *Tanzimat* reformers of the 19th century attempted to integrate what they considered the best parts of modernising European civilisation, such as centralisation and patriotism, reform of the army and economic development while maintaining the pre-eminence of the Ottoman dynasty and Islam. The nominally Ottoman-controlled, but to all intents and purposes independent, Egypt of Muhammad Ali (1769–1849) was the most enthusiastic Islamic embracer of modernisation. Muhammad Ali challenged Ottoman control of the Arab Middle East and occupied Syria from 1831 to 1840 before being forced to withdraw by the Great Powers. The restoration of Ottoman power in Syria saw increased Ottoman attempts to deepen their control over the region. Consequently, the Ottoman state greatly expanded its involvement in society in the lives of its citizens.[5] Modernisation, as slowly as it developed in the Fertile Crescent and Arabia, brought with it the growth of urban areas throughout the Ottoman Middle East such as Beirut, Damascus, Aleppo and Baghdad, breaking down the traditional ties of tribe and family that tended to dominate relationships in the Arab world.

Nationalism in the Arab Middle East before 1914

For many years, it was widely accepted that Arab nationalism, in its early stages, arose from contact with the West. Unsurprisingly the first signs of a distinctively Arab nationalism begin to emerge in the urban areas of Ottoman Syria, where European and American cultural and educational influence was beginning to grow in the late 19th century in tandem with increased Western political and economic penetration of the region. European and American missionary work was linked to the Holy Places in Palestine but also by a desire, especially among Protestant congregations, to convert Muslims. Direct proselytisation was illegal but there seems to have been a vague, and ultimately forlorn, hope that Arab Christians might transmit their faith to Muslims.[6] A handful of Syrian Christians, educated in the American and French missionary schools in the Lebanon that were established in the 19th century, began to develop a quasi-secular Arab nationalism. This included the revival of many classical Arabic literary texts and the translating of Western texts into Arabic. In the 1860s a Syrian Christian, Ibrahim al-Yaziji, articulated an early vision of Arab nationalism. He viewed the Ottoman conquest as a disaster for the Arabs who had regressed from being a technically-advanced and learned civilisation to one that remained mired in backwardness and more interested in religion than science. Throwing off the Ottoman yoke, in his view, would allow the Arabs to resume their previous trajectory of learning and advancement. However, this secular vision of Arab nationalism was anathema to the vast bulk of Muslim Arabs, who remained committed to, or at least dispassionate about, the Ottoman Empire.[7]

George Antonius, in his 1938 book *The Arab Awakening*, perhaps the key text of modern Arab nationalism, saw the genesis of Arab nationalism within these very small cultural movements in late 19th century Ottoman Syria. Since the Second World War, there has been increasing scepticism regarding some of Antonius's claims regarding the origins of Arab nationalism and his account of the Arab Revolt during the First World War.[8] Even a sympathetic observer notes that it is not only 'a work of historical narrative, but also of political advocacy'.[9] Relying essentially on oral evidence, Antonius almost certainly overplayed the role of a small Lebanese grouping, the Secret Society, which distributed placards agitating against the Ottomans in the late 1870. This agitation, it is likely, was more to do with particular local factors involving Maronite Christians than the genesis of an Arab nationalism aimed against the Turks.[10]

Some 30 years later there were more concrete signs of a nascent Arab nationalism. The spur was the 1908 Young Turk revolution in Constantinople. In 1878 the Sultan had abrogated the Ottoman constitution that he had been forced to enact by the European powers. Afterwards groups in the army and within the civil administration sought the restoration of constitutional rule and the placing of the Empire on a more liberal and modern footing. The most notable of these were the Ottoman Freedom Society and the Committee of Union and Progress (CUP). In July 1908, these groups, collectively known as the Young Turks, seized power. Reform-minded nationalist officers linked to the CUP emerged as the dominant force in the new regime. Arab reaction was initially enthusiastic. The initial phase of liberalism delivered by the CUP saw political activity permitted in the Empire including the formation of specifically Arab parties. Soon it became clear that the Young Turks' flirtation with liberalism and pluralism was merely a veneer behind which lurked a Turkish

George Habib Antonius (1891–1942), was a British colonial administrator and Arab nationalist historian. Born in the Lebanon to a prosperous Greek Orthodox Christian family, he lived in Egypt before taking a degree at Cambridge. He joined the British-administered Egyptian government just before the outbreak of the First World War, serving in various administrative jobs during the War before becoming translator for Emir Feisal at the Peace Conference in 1919. In 1921, he joined the British Colonial Office, and became a senior official in the Palestinian administration before resigning in May 1930 for a variety of political and personal reasons. In 1931, ex-King Hussein provided him with key source material for his seminal work on Arab nationalism, *The Arab Awakening* (1938). This published, for the first time, the correspondence between Hussein and Henry McMahon, which Antonius claimed demonstrated British betrayal of the Arab cause.[11]

nationalist agenda, which reinforced tendencies towards centralisation and Turkification already evident in the Ottoman
Empire. Indeed there is little evidence that the Young Turks
drove forward these policies to any greater extent than the old
regime had.[12] However, by briefly opening up the Ottoman
policy, they made it harder to go back to the old authoritarian system.

After 1912, in a reaction to the end of the period of reform,
parties with an agenda of Arab autonomy began to emerge in
Syria. The most important of these, according to Antonius,
was the Decentralisation Party. Other bodies of importance,
again in Syria, were secret societies with similar manifestos
including *al-Fatat* (the Young Arab Society) and *al-Qahtan-
yia*. Antonius would seek later to link these groupings into the
Hashemite revolt against the Ottomans from 1916, thereby
creating a bond between the more urban-based nationalism
of the streets of Damascus and the arid deserts from which
the Hashemites sprang.

According to its critics, however, Antonius's vision of the
origins and development of Arab nationalism was exaggerated
and fallacious. The pro-independence or autonomy-minded
Arabs of Syria were a tiny minority, numbering around 350
members according to a recent authoritative survey,[13] and
Hashemite ambitions were nearly all to do with their own
aggrandisement rather than a high-minded commitment to
Arab nationalism.[14] The dominant scholarly interpretation of
the origins of Arab nationalism is C Ernest Dawn's hypothesis
that the stirrings of Arab nationalism in the early part of the
20th century emerged not from Western-influenced Christian
Arabs but from reform-minded Muslims in the religious elite.
It also arose from the conflict among the Arab notables and
the elite particularly in the major cities such as Damascus.

Those who held favour, land and office due to Ottoman patronage tended to support the *status quo* while those excluded from this spoils system began to agitate against it.[15] Even among the recalcitrant, there was little desire for complete independence. Most Arabs would have been content to 'remain within the frame of the Ottoman unity, as long as their proper place was recognised by the Turkish rulers'.[16]

There were also enormous differences between city and countryside. Writing nearly 90 years ago, the influential English Arabist Gertrude Bell was perhaps closer than Antonius to the true state of Arab nationalism around the early years of the 20th century

> 'There is no nation of Arabs; the Syrian merchant is separated by a wider gulf from the bedouin than he is from the Osmanli [Ottoman] ...'
> **GERTRUDE BELL**

when she wrote: 'There is no nation of Arabs; the Syrian merchant is separated by a wider gulf from the bedouin than he is from the Osmanli [Ottoman] ...'[17] At the beginning of the 20th century national politics in Syria remained 'an urban game largely isolated from village needs and wishes'.[18]

The Hejaz

The Hejaz is a narrow strip of land that extends from just south of what is now the Jordanian port of Aquba to nearly as far as the northern border of the Yemen. It now lies within the Kingdom of Saudi Arabia, though at the outbreak of the First World War it was a *vilayet* or province of the Ottoman Empire. Indeed it was practically the only part of the Arabian Peninsula where the writ of the Ottomans ran at all. Situated on a barren and inhospitable stretch of coastline, its importance lay in the fact that two of the holiest sites of Islam lay within it: Mecca, the holiest city, and Medina, the first city

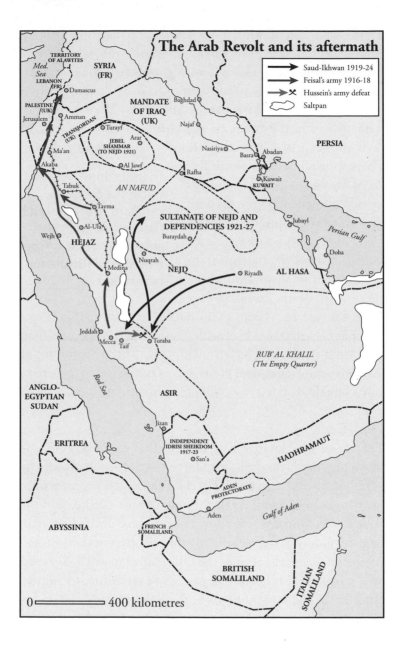

The Arab Revolt and its aftermath

→	Saud-Ikhwan 1919-24
→	Feisal's army 1916-18
→✕	Hussein's army defeat
	Saltpan

TERRITORY
OF ALAWITES

Med.
Sea

LEBANON
(FR)

SYRIA
(FR)

PALESTINE
(UK)

Damascus

Baghdad

MANDATE
OF IRAQ
(UK)

Jerusalem

Amman

TRANSJORDAN
(UK)

Turayf

Arar

Najaf

PERSIA

Ma'an

JEBEL
SHAMMAR
(TO NEJD 1921)

Nasiriya

Basra

Abadan

Akaba

Al Jawf

Rafha

Kuwait

KUWAIT

Tabuk

AN NAFUD

Tayma

Al-Ula

SULTANATE OF NEJD AND
DEPENDENCIES 1921-27

Jubayl

Persian Gulf

Wejh

HEJAZ

Buraydah

Doha

Nuqrah

Medina

NEJD

Riyadh

AL HASA

Jeddah

Mecca

Taif

Turaba

RUB' AL KHALIL
(The Empty Quarter)

ANGLO-
EGYPTIAN
SUDAN

Red Sea

ASIR

ERITREA

Jizan

INDEPENDENT
IDRISI SHEIKDOM
1917-23

San'a

HADHRAMAUT

ADEN
PROTECTORATE

Aden

Gulf of Aden

ABYSSINIA

FRENCH
SOMALILAND

BRITISH
SOMALILAND

ITALIAN
SOMALILAND

0 ▭▭▭▭▭ 400 kilometres

to accept the word of Prophet Muhammad. It was remote from the capital Constantinople, poor and thinly populated. Indeed, it is estimated that towards the end of the 19th century, the combined population of the three main towns of the Hejaz – Mecca, Medina and Jeddah – was little more than 100,000 with perhaps another 400,000 nomadic tribesman in the hinterland around them.[19] The territory lacked natural resources and much of the urban population was devoted to the study and practice of religion. Its main source of income was the influx of pilgrims from all corners of the Muslim world, who as part of their religious duty as Muslims were compelled, at least once in their life, to make the annual *Hajj* to the Holy Places at Mecca. The presence of the holiest cities of Islam within the Hejaz conferred considerable benefits upon the area. It was not subject to conscription or normal levels of Ottoman taxation. Indeed, it tended to be a net recipient of aid from Constantinople, as well as receiving subventions from relatively wealthy Muslim states such as Egypt. It has been argued that 'religion determined the social, economic, and, to a lesser degree, the political history of western Arabia [ie, the Hejaz] in the nineteenth century'.[20] It remained a pre-modern, highly traditional society. There were little outward signs of nationalism or other modern political ideas permeating the area during the 19th century.[21]

The Hashemites

Nearly 13 centuries after the death of the Prophet, those who were descended from him, were entitled to use the title Sherif. (Sherif is usually translated as eminent, distinguished or noble.) These Sherifians were, as Jan Morris describes them, 'halfway between a priesthood and nobility'.[22] Among the most important of these Sherifian families was the House of Beni Hashem (hence 'Hashemites'), from the Prophet's Quraysh tribe. Sherif Hussein ibn Ali of the Hashemites filled the most important position in the Hejaz, the Grand Sherif and Emir of Mecca, from 1908. Hussein's branch of the Hashemites was raised out of relative obscurity when, during the 19th century Muhammad Ali, the ruler of Egypt, had ruled the Hejaz and installed Hussein's grandfather as Grand Sherif and Emir of Mecca.[23] The power that came with this position tended to be more religious than political and there is little evidence before the beginning of the 20th century that the Hashemites showed any great political ambitions. Though Arab, the Hashemites were also part of the Ottoman establishment. The independence of the Grand Sherifs was circumscribed by the presence of a Turkish governor or *Vali* in Mecca and the presence of some 7,000 troops. However, communications with Constantinople before the completion of the Hejaz railway in 1908 were slow and difficult, and distance from the imperial capital generally allowed the Emir of Mecca a reasonable degree of autonomy. There was little tax collection and no conscription due to the Hejaz's sacred status. However, as one writer in the 19th century stated, the Emir of Mecca was a 'mere creature of the Porte, removable at the pleasure of the Sultan. Besides, he has no influence whatever, political or spiritual, beyond his own assigned district.'[24] Indeed the ultimate control of the Ottomans over the Hashemites and Hejaz was demonstrated by the practice of bringing important members of leading families of the Hejaz, such as the Hashemites, to Constantinople as enforced guests of the Sultan.

However, it should also be borne in mind that Ottoman rule and the Turkish garrison also afforded a degree of security for the Hejaz. The Arabian Peninsula was a dangerous place with plenty of tribes and religious rivals (the Imam of Yemen, the Wahhabis and by the early 20th century the rising power of Ibn Saud) seeking to extend their influence. Since 1800 the British had been busy securing key positions and acquiring allies amongst the various Emirs on the coastal peripheries of the peninsula. The British presence and influence was most apparent at the southern end of the Red Sea at Aden, and in the Persian Gulf. Its aim was to protect the key sea route to British India.[25]

The Caliphate

Abdülhamid II, the Ottoman Sultan, (r. 1876–1909), was also Caliph, the protector of the religion of Islam and the Holy Places. His predecessors since Sultan Suleyman the Magnificent (r. 1520–66) had been acknowledged as such by the Islamic World. However, when Abdülhamid II assumed the title of Caliph, there was opposition voiced by some. Some were proto-Arab nationalists who demanded the restoration of an Arab Caliphate. Some prophetic traditions, of admittedly dubious origin, claimed that the Caliphate could only be held by members of the Prophet's own tribe, 'the Quraysh'. Others were British government officials – many in the India Office and Indian Civil Service – who did not like the Ottoman Sultan having such potential influence over the near 100 million Muslims in British India. One retired British civil servant suggested the Hashemite Emir of Mecca, a member of the Quraysh, would be a more pliable Caliph of Islam 'for he lives by the side of our road to India and would be as completely in our power as the Suez Canal'.[26] It was a prescient comment.

The Rise of Sherif Hussein[27]

Hussein ibn Ali was born in 1853 in Constantinople. Half Circassian, half Arab, his family connections to the Aoun clan, a branch of the Hashemites, were what made him important, as he was 37th in the line of descent from the Prophet.[28] There were approximately 800 members of the rival Aoun and Zaid clans who could claim this sacred lineage. At various times, one branch or the other would be ascendant and would hold the title of Emir or Grand Sherif of Mecca. In the 1880s and 1890s, the Zaid branch was dominant. At the time of the outbreak of the First World War, Hussein was over 60. Nonetheless, he was a striking looking, black-robed, turban-clad figure with an almost snow-white beard. T E Lawrence, the British army officer who would have key role in the Arab Revolt, describes him as 'outwardly so clean and gentle-mannered as to seem weak; but this appearance hid a crafty policy, deep ambition, and an un-Arabian foresight, strength of character and obstinacy'.[29] He was in many respects a charismatic figure, learned in Arab literature and familiar with the intrigues of international diplomacy. His Ottoman upbringing had also bred some rather unattractive qualities in the Sherif. According to Lawrence: 'Hussein when young had been honest, outspoken ... [but] he learned not merely to suppress his speech, but to use speech to conceal his honest purpose. The art, over-indulged, became a vice from which he could not free himself.'[30]

> 'Hussein when young had been honest, outspoken ... [but] he learned not merely to suppress his speech, but to use speech to conceal his honest purpose. The art, over-indulged, became a vice from which he could not free himself.'
>
> **T E LAWRENCE**

His early years are shrouded in mystery. We do know that a leading scion of the Hashemite family, he was an enforced guest of the Sultan for more than 15 years from 1892 or 1893 to 1908. His confinement, if it could be even called that, was extremely benign. The Sultan, not wishing to be accused of treating a Sherifian badly, had Hussein, his wife and four sons, Ali (1879–1935), Abdullah (1880–1951), Feisal (1883–1933) and Zeid (1898–1970), established in a comfortable villa on the Bosporus. Three of the four sons (Ali, Abdullah and Feisal) were to become kings of three of the successor states of the Ottoman Empire (see page 22).

Hussein became a prominent citizen in Constantinople, and was, in many respects, assimilated into the Ottoman way of life. Turkish appears to have come as easily to him as Arabic. Hussein, though, was extremely strong-willed and independent minded and was probably too dangerous a figure to have ever been left to return to the Hejaz by the despotic Sultan Abdülhamid II.[31] However, events intervened. When the Young Turks assumed power in 1908, Abdülhamid's powers were truncated and he was deposed after a year. The position of Grand Sherif of Mecca fell vacant around the same time as the revolution, thanks to the deposition of the holder Sherif Ali Abdullah ibn Muhammad and the sudden death of his successor. Hussein was a leading candidate for the position, though his succession was by no means a formality. He was helped by his political views and an ability to ingratiate himself with key players. A deeply reactionary figure in many respects, he was not an admirer of the Young Turks. His hostility to the new government may well have attracted Abdülhamid to Hussein's candidature. There is also some evidence that the British government viewed him as a suitable candidate, thanks to Hussein's own timely overtures to the

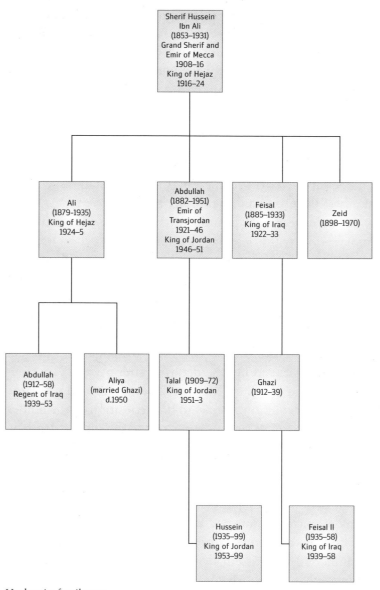

Hashemite family tree

British Ambassador to Constantinople, in which he claimed to have written to influence Arab chiefs in the Hejaz to favour British interests in the Arabian Peninsula.[32] Abdülhamid may have hoped to attract British support at a time when his position was under increasing pressure from the CUP. Abdülhamid also viewed the Caliphate and the loyalty this engendered amongst his Islamic subjects as a key element in his survival. It was in his interests therefore to have a figure opposed to the Young Turks in the important position of Grand Sherif of Mecca. Hussein, according to his son Abdullah, pledged that if the CUP made life too difficult for Abdülhamid, he could have asylum in the Hejaz.[33]

Hussein as Sherif and the Ottomans

In 1908 Hussein was made Sherif and returned to the Hejaz. However, there is some evidence that once he had done so, Hussein raised his sights and began to contemplate that he, not the Ottoman Sultan, should be Caliph. His son Abdullah testifies in his memoirs that Hussein was loyal to the Ottomans at this time and his main argument with Constantinople was the secularising reforms of the CUP. In his view, the Young Turks, 'were ill advised when they converted the Imperial Caliphate administration into a racial "Constitutional" Government and replaced the Islamic and therefore ultimately Arab supervision of the State by a Western juridical control'.[34] In contrast to this, right from the beginning of his reign, Hussein made clear that traditional Islamic law, the *Sharia*, was what guided him.[35] Hussein's priority upon arrival in the Hejaz was to consolidate his power base and increase his influence at the expense of the Turkish *Vali*. Indeed, by 1911 the British were reporting that Hussein had completely outmaneuvered the various *Vali* sent there and the government of Mecca was essentially in his hands. A British despatch from 1914 reported that on his arrival in 1908, Hussein had 'created a good impression, and it was hoped that he would not prove extortionate and would restore security in the country about Mecca'. After initial clamping down on brigandage, Hussein appears to have tolerated it. The British consul in Mecca reported that the murderers of three Indian pilgrims had links to the Grand Sherif.[36]

However, Hussein needed to be circumspect in his challenges to the various *Vali* and Ottoman authorities. For going too far could lead to his deposition. Indeed his earliest achievement was to bring the increasingly fractious Bedouin tribes adjacent to the Hejaz under control. The Ottomans, who after 1910 had much greater military priorities in the Balkans and in Libya, encouraged Hussein to extend his power into eastern Arabia and to assert Ottoman control against the two independent tribal leaders Ibn Saud and the Idrisi of 'Asir. According to the British consul in Jeddah, Hussein viewed these campaigns as a means by which he could consolidate his own power and autonomy.[37] But the tentacles of Ottoman and Turkish control over the Hejaz were beginning to grow, not wither, in the period immediately before the First World War. Telegraph wires linked the Hejaz to Constantinople from the end of the 19th century and by 1908, communications were revolutionised by the completion of the Hejaz railway that linked Damascus to the city of Medina and the other Holy Places. The railway was greeted with considerable hostility by the Bedouin tribes of the Hejaz, who viewed the 'Iron Donkey' as a serious threat to their main sources of income: the guiding, transportation and occasional robbing of pilgrims. Significantly, the Young Turks appear to have viewed the railway and its eventual extension to Mecca as the cornerstone of the consolidation of more direct Ottoman rule in western Arabia. Indeed Medina, the town at the end of the railway line, began to come under much greater Ottoman influence in the years up to 1914. Hussein, upon his installation as Sherif, encouraged attacks on the trains and he assiduously resisted entreaties from the Young Turks to extend the line down to his power base at Mecca.[38]

It is clear, however, that Hussein's autonomy in the years leading up to the outbreak of the First World War was becoming increasingly circumscribed. His son, Abdullah, complained about the tyranny of the Turks to the French Ambassador in 1912 and around this time, the first tentative contacts between Abdullah and the British may have taken place.[39] The key event in the deterioration of the Hashemite position was the installation of Vehib Bey as the *Vali* from April 1914. Made of much more formidable stuff than his predecessors, he soon began clipping Hussein's wings. Vehib was determined that the dual control over the Hejaz would end and more direct Ottoman rule be established. Hashemite supporters in the administration were summarily dismissed and replaced by Ottoman placemen. Abdullah's contacts with the British, seeking their support for autonomy for the Hejaz in February and April 1914 appear to have been directly motivated by the growing pressure being placed on his father by Vehib.[40] It is clear that Ibn Saud, Hussein's great rival for supremacy in Arabia, who was also subject to Ottoman sovereignty, had far more autonomy in the isolated Nejd territories of central Arabia. Sherif Hussein ran the risk that if he pushed matters too far in his defiance of the Turkish government he could find himself removed from office.

Hussein's clashes with the Ottomans were very much related to his own desires for self-aggrandisement and protection from the increasing encroachments on his powers by Ottoman officials. His Arab nationalist credentials were 'questionable'.[41] Indeed, there is little evidence of any significant Arab nationalist pressures in the Hejaz. Within the socio-economic makeup of the region there were none of the key groupings (journalists, army officers and intellectuals) that were present at the creation of other nationalisms.[42] To speak of 'nationalism' in the Hejaz, therefore, is a misnomer. The Arab Revolt, there at least, sprang almost entirely from a clash over power between the Hashemites, who considered themselves an elite whose privileges and autonomy were being threatened, and the Ottomans, who wanted to forge a modern centralised state. If the Ottomans had shown more skill in handling Hussein, the Sherif would have been most unlikely to lead a revolt against the Ottomans. The revolution in international politics brought about by the First World War, especially the willingness of all powers to support persons or groupings with grievances within their enemies' territories for subversive purposes, would provide Hussein with the means to take advantage of a unique opportunity to expand his power.

2
The First World War and the Rise of Arab Nationalism

Turkey enters the war

The decision of the upper echelons of the Turkish leadership to go to war in 1914 doomed the Ottoman Empire. It would appear that the majority of the Ottoman leadership was initially in favour of sitting out the war or at least maintaining neutrality until it was clear which side – the Central Powers (Germany and Austria) or the Triple Entente (France, Britain and Russia) – was going to emerge victorious. They then hoped to exchange their support for territorial gains in the Aegean, North Africa and Asia Minor. The principle policy-makers were CUP leaders among whom War Minister Enver Pasha (1881–1922), and Interior Minister Mehmed Talât (1874–1921) were the first amongst equals.[1] This group was far more enthusiastic about forging an alliance with the Central Powers than other cabinet members. Enver, especially, was anxious to restore the Ottoman Empire's power by means of joint military action with Germany. It was he who took the initiative in sheltering and the reflagging under the Ottoman ensign two German warships, *Goeben* and *Breslau*, early in August 1914. Then, he authorised the German commander and crews of these ships to bombard Russian bases on the Black Sea – the event that led the Entente to declare war on Ottoman Turkey in November 1914.

At first the Entente Powers were not overly concerned about Ottoman entry into the war. The Ottoman armies had performed poorly in the Balkan Wars of 1912–13. Italy, in contrast, appeared to be a much more significant military force than the Turks, which was why the Entente vigorously wooed it. Secondly, the Ottoman Empire offered plenty of opportunities for territorial aggrandisement for each of the Entente Powers. However, matters did not turn out as the Entente might have hoped. Turkey proved to be a formidable and doughty opponent able to inflict stinging reverses on the British and French at Gallipoli in 1915 and on the British at Kut in Eastern Mesopotamia in 1916. In no sense was Turkey the soft underbelly of the Central Powers.

Britain and the Ottoman Empire

During the 19th century Britain was the most ardent advocate amongst the Great Powers of maintaining the territorial integrity of the Ottoman Empire. Its key objective was the protection of British land and sea routes to India and it believed a weak Turkey straddling these routes was infinitely preferable to Russia holding this position, which seemed the most likely outcome of the dissolution and partition of the Empire. In order to preserve Turkey, Britain sought to promote liberalisation and modernisation in the Ottoman regime. Without internal reform, the Empire would probably collapse – either splitting into competing nationalities (Slavs, Turks and Arabs) or more likely being partitioned between the Great Powers. For much of the 19th century, the British feared that it would be the Russians who would gain the lion's share of any such partition. Britain, therefore, tended to support the Ottoman Empire against Russian military and political pressure in the Balkans but also in Asia Minor. In 1854–6, Britain, together with France, fought the Crimean War on behalf of Turkey against Russia. Once more, in 1878, Britain came close to war over Russia's attempt to impose the Carthaginian Peace of San Stefano on Turkey, which would have seen the virtual end of the Ottoman Empire in Europe, following the Russo-Turkish War of 1877. At a hastily arranged Congress of the Great Powers at Berlin in 1878, much of this was reversed though Turkey still lost substantial territory in Europe.

However, 1878 marked a watershed in British policy. Hitherto, British support did not cost the Ottomans anything. After 1878 this began to change. Along with the other powers, Britain agreed to the severe diminution of Turkey's possessions in Europe at the Congress of Berlin. Independence was granted to Romania, Serbia and Montenegro, autonomy granted to Bulgaria and Bosnia handed over to Austrian administration. Even the British support for Turkey at the Congress of Berlin was garnered only at the price of the island of Cyprus for use as a British base. In 1882, Britain occupied Egypt and the strategic Suez Canal. While Egypt had been practically independent since the early 19th century, the Ottoman Sultan remained nominal sovereign. However, the British after 1882 showed a marked reluctance to withdraw from Egypt and ignored Ottoman rights. Britain also refused to end the humiliating Capitulations imposed on Turkey, which gave foreign citizens extensive exemptions from Turkish laws and taxes. Britain, in many respects, had by the end of the 19th century begun to display as much avarice

The Ottoman Empire 1914

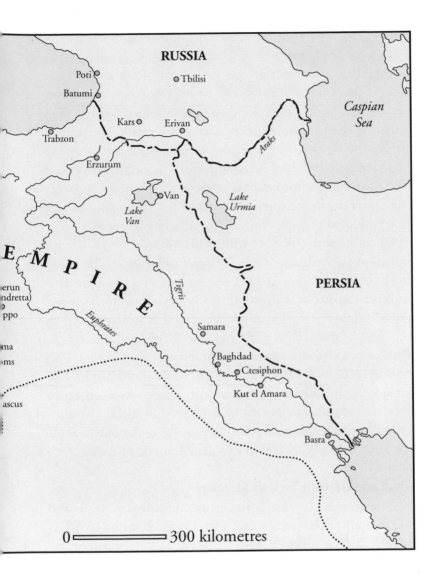

about certain parts of the crumbling edifice of the Ottoman Empire as any other power. From the mid 1890s, but especially in the aftermath of the 1907 Anglo-Russian Entente, Britain became more relaxed about Russian ambitions towards Turkey though she would have preferred that a final partition of the Empire be avoided. As a result, the decade before the First World War had seen 'the almost complete abandonment by her of her traditional Turcophil policy ...'.[2] The British remained intent that should the Empire collapse, their interests in the southern flank of the Ottoman Empire, that straddled the route to India, would be protected.[3]

Upon the outbreak of hostilities in November 1914, Britain moved swiftly to secure key strategic objectives. The existing garrison in Egypt at Suez was strengthened and the pro-Turkish Khedive was deposed. An Indian (later to be called the Mesopotamian) Expeditionary Force was dispatched to the head of the Persian Gulf to secure British oil interests in Persia from Ottoman attack and to protect the various Arab princes, such as the Emir of Kuwait, with whom Britain had already established treaty relationships. A lesser objective was to secure the co-operation of other Arab allies. The most powerful figures in the Arabian Peninsula at the outbreak of the First World War were Ibn Saud and Sherif Hussein.

Jihad and German Turkish Strategy

The urgent requirement to secure additional Arab and Muslim allies was reinforced with the declaration of *Jihad* ('Holy War') against the Entente by the Sultan of Turkey on 14 November 1914, calling on all loyal Muslim believers to rise up against the British, the French and the Russians. The Kaiser had appealed to Enver to do this in August 1914 even before Ottoman entry into the war. The Germans viewed the

Entente Powers' colonial empires as providing both potential dangers and opportunities for the Central Powers. In a
long war, the Entente would be able to mobilise manpower,
raw materials and other resources from these possessions.
However, if Germany could ferment latent nationalist, religious and ethnic tensions in her opponents' empires in Africa
and Asia, the value of their colonies to the war effort could be
severely diminished. Trouble in the British Empire, in particular, could provide the seeds of victory for the Central Powers.
In 1908, a German official suggested to the then German
Chancellor that in the event of a war, 'if Turkey participates
against England, one may certainly expect an overall revolt of
the Muslims in the British colonies'. This would tie down the
British army and much of the navy.[4] Arthur Zimmermann,
the Germany Deputy Foreign Minister, was enthusiastic
about using Turkey and pan-Islamism to ferment uprisings
against the British, French and the Russians. Even if a call to
Jihad was only a partial success, it could still be a cause of
serious disruption to the Allies. There were some 70 million
Muslims in India and 16 million in Egypt and the Sudan
under direct British control along with 20 million in French
Africa, and similar numbers of adherents within Russia's
borders. Enver, the architect of Turkey's entry into the War,
shared these views and planned to use pan-Turkish ideology
to inflame the Turkish populations of the Caucasus against
the Russians and pan-Islamic ideology to inflame Egypt and
Muslim areas of India against the British. The British, in particular, were desperately concerned that the Turkish Sultan
would proclaim a *Jihad*, for fear it would work. Now pre-war
contacts that the British had with both Sherif Hussein and
Ibn Saud took on an unexpected importance. If the British
could engineer a split in the Muslim world and cast doubt on

the verisimilitude of the Sultan's declaration, its effects could be mitigated.

Initial British contacts with the Hashemites

In February 1914, Sherif Hussein's second son Abdullah, who was a member of the Ottoman Parliament in Constantinople, had paid a visit to the British High Commissioner in Egypt, Field Marshal Lord Kitchener. The visit was, to all intents and purposes, a courtesy call. However, Abdullah took the opportunity to tell Kitchener that there was a growing crisis in the Hejaz between the Sherif and the new Turkish *Vali*. He requested British support in event of an attempt to depose his father. Specifically he asked that they use their influence with Constantinople and block Turkish troops from being transported through the Suez Canal.[5] This support, which was unlikely to have been granted, was not needed. It was soon reported that the differences between Hussein and the Turks had been settled amicably.[6] However, the British continued to hear of persistent rumours of dissatisfaction in the Ottoman Arab world. At a subsequent meeting in April 1914 with the Oriental Secretary to the British Residency in Cairo, Ronald Storrs, at the Khedive's palace in Cairo, Abdullah reported that negotiations in Constantinople had not gone well and his father had requested that he ask the British government to enter into a quasi-protectorate with the Emir of Mecca that would forestall any Turkish aggression. There was no prospect of this in April 1914. Britain's relations with the Ottoman Empire, while not having the warmth of hitherto, remained fundamentally correct. The following day, after consulting Kitchener, Storrs told Abdullah he could not expect any British support though Elie Kedourie suggests that the rejection was not as categorical as it seemed.[7] However,

Storrs, Kitchener, the Governor-General of the Sudan, Reginald Wingate, and the intelligence department in the British-run Egyptian War Office all appear to have recognised that the situation in Arabia in 1914 afforded opportunities for the British government to exploit should the Ottomans go to war against the Entente.

Kitchener, who had stayed in London at the outbreak of hostilities to become Secretary of State for War, ordered Storrs to reactivate contacts with Abdullah in September 1914 as it became increasingly evident that Turkey was likely to enter the war on the side of the Central Powers. He was to ascertain the attitude of Sherif Hussein should hostilities break out between the Entente and Turkey. Abdullah, in a guarded reply, agreed that the Hashemite position was essentially favourable to the British, though it appeared that there would be no outright rebellion against the Ottomans unless they struck first to circumscribe the independence of Hussein. The British replied that they would protect Hussein against aggression but also raised the tantalising possibility that a favorable outcome of the war might include the replacement of the Ottoman Sultan as Caliph by an Arab figure.[8] Storrs, who was ordered to transmit the reply, may have greatly exceeded his instructions from London, promising much more wide-ranging support to Hussein and the Arab cause than he was authorised to give.[9] Hussein, on 8 December 1914, replied that he could not break with the Ottomans at present but would do so should a suitable moment arrive. He also stated that 'there no longer exists a Caliphate ... for their [the Ottomans'] rule projects ... deeds that are all contrary to religion. The Caliphate means this, that the rule of the book of God should be enforced, and this they do not do.'[10]

Storrs seems to have taken further local initiatives without referring to London, which committed Britain almost completely to the general cause of Arab nationalism and an Arab Caliphate. Most notably, in December 1914 he issued a sweeping Proclamation from the Government of Great Britain to the natives of Arabia and the Arab provinces, pledging support for Arab independence and declaring that the Caliphate was the right of a member of the Quraysh, i.e. someone like Sherif Hussein.[11] This was followed by another assurance issued to the Arabs in April 1915 pledging to support Arab independence and declaring British opposition to annexations by any of the Great Powers in the Holy Places or the Arabian Peninsula. These British assurances appear to have done enough to keep Hussein in play. He did not endorse the Caliph's call for *Jihad*; instead he maintained a pointed silence on the matter. This was, in itself, a considerable gain for the British. Had Hussein enthusiastically endorsed the Sultan's proclamation of 14 November 1914, this would have greatly enhanced its impact with the attendant possibility of undermining the British position in Egypt and India.

Entente Politics and the Middle East

At the same time as Storrs was taking his initiatives, the Entente Powers – Britain, France and Russia – were negotiating over the fate of the Ottoman Empire. It was clear that they now all desired to turn the 'sick man of Europe' into a corpse, which they could dissect in the aftermath of victory. Furthermore, Britain, after the initial bloody but inconclusive battles of 1914 on the Eastern and Western Fronts, believed that keeping Russia in the War was now the most important aim of British wartime diplomacy. The Ottoman entry into the war was useful from this perspective as its territory could be parceled out, without too many qualms, as an incentive to keep Russia in the War. In November 1914, the British and French informed the Russians that they would have no objection to them taking possession of the Bosphorus and the Dardanelles, which link the Mediterranean and the Black Sea. When the British and French attacked the Dardanelles in 1915, Russia demanded firmer assurances and in the Constantinople Agreement (March 1915), it was promised Constantinople and the Straits if the War ended successfully.[12]

Ironically, it was France rather than Britain which objected to this.[13] Both powers now felt that should Russia gain this fantastic prize – the goal of Russian statesmen since the reign of Peter the Great – they would need to be compensated by significant territorial gains in other parts of the Ottoman Empire. France had its own shopping list of territories: Cilicia, Syria and Palestine. In March 1915, Edward Grey, the Secretary of State for Foreign Affairs, asked the War Council of the British Cabinet to consider whether Britain should establish another Islamic state to placate Muslim opinion in India concerned by the potential destruction of the Ottoman Empire. In Grey's view the only possible location for this territory was in Arabia, Mesopotamia and Syria.

Kitchener, in a remarkably prescient paper also in March 1915, proposed that 'it is to our interests to see an Arab Kingdom established in Arabia under the auspices of England, bounded in the north by the Valley of the Tigris and Euphrates and containing within it the chief Mahomedan Holy Places, Mecca, Medina and Kerbala'. Kitchener believed that in the aftermath of victory, Russia's position in the Middle East would be immeasurably strengthened and that Britain needed to think of acquiring territory or influence from the Mediterranean to the Persian Gulf to protect the route to India. Indeed, Kitchener gave serious consideration to the construction of a railroad from Alexandretta on the Mediterranean coast to Basra at the head of the Gulf on which British forces could be rapidly deployed to reinforce the India garrison. There was a general disagreement in the Cabinet as to what Britain should seek. Asquith, while sharing Grey's disquiet about a territorial carve-up, concluded that if a scramble for Ottoman possessions took place, Britain would be neglecting its duty if it did not seek something for itself. [14]

An interdepartmental committee, the de Bunsen Committee[15] was established in April 1915 tasked with identifying British territorial interests in a post-war settlement. Rather than an outright partition of Asiatic Turkey, it recommended that spheres of influence were preferable though it carefully drew up four maps that included two variations based on outright annexation, one for spheres of influence and one where modern-day Syria and Iraq as well as Palestine and an Armenian entity received devolution as part of a decentralisation scheme for the Ottoman Empire. It was envisaged under all these schemes that an independent Arab state would be established in the Arabian Peninsula. British Eastern policy remained confused because there was no single voice speaking on the matter. Twenty Departments or Offices of State had input in London, while civil servants in Cairo and Delhi as well as local military commanders had the power to run their own foreign policies, often it would appear, with little or no clearance from London. Gauging the British position on the future of the Middle East during the War was difficult, if not impossible, for the British themselves, let alone for their prospective allies such as the Hashemites.

Anglo-Arab negotiations 1915

In January 1915, Sir Henry McMahon became High Commissioner to Egypt in succession to Kitchener. He began taking tentative soundings on how to encourage the Arabs to split with the Ottomans. In the east and centre of the Arabian Peninsula the British were enjoying considerable success in acquiring support from the smaller Arab tribal rulers: the Emir of Kuwait, Ibn Saud, then ruler of Nejd and the Idrisi of 'Asir had all been brought firmly into the British orbit by mid-1915. At the same time, Hussein was coming under growing pressure from the Turks to openly support the Caliph's call for *Jihad*. Indeed, he was showing considerable support for it in theory, though in practice this amounted to little more than the staging of a few demonstrations. Instead Hussein emphasised to the Turks the vulnerability of the coast of the Hejaz to British attacks from Egypt and the Sudan. In secret, though, Hussein was plotting bolder moves – an alliance with the British. The motivation for this is unclear. It is claimed that Hussein's main ambition was to become Caliph and there is little evidence of his Arabism at this point.[16] A key factor in motivating his disillusionment with the Ottomans appears to have been his uncovering in January 1915 of a plot to unseat him by the CUP. Only the outbreak of war had prevented its implementation.

In March 1915, Hussein, still inclined to seek compromise with the Turks, sent his son Feisal with the incriminating documents to the Grand Vizier in Constantinople. This may have been an elaborate subterfuge to allow Feisal to make contact in Damascus with the Arab nationalist groupings *al-Fatat* and *al-Ahd*. However, Feisal's initial impressions of these groupings were that they were insufficiently strong to revolt against the Ottomans without the support of outside powers.[17] Feisal proceeded onto Constantinople. Here, he stayed for a month attempting to reach agreement with the Turkish government over the issue of the plot against his father. The leading figures in the government, the Sultan, the Grand Vizier, Talât and Enver all disavowed any knowledge and promised to transfer the Turkish governor. However, the Turks also made clear that they would not go any further to strengthen Hussein's position until he fully endorsed and declared *Jihad* against the British. Feisal promised loyalty to the Sultan and agreed to provide forces to help the upcoming Turkish attack on Suez. However, this was a tissue of lies. In reality, he was deeply dissatisfied with the Turks and confirmed in his view that the present situation could not continue.

On his way back to the Hejaz in May 1915, Feisal stopped off in Damascus to consult with the nationalists. They had been grievously weakened since their last meeting by a Turkish crackdown. Many of the Arab-manned Ottoman divisions in the Fertile Crescent had been broken up and their troops sent to the fronts at Gallipoli and the Caucasus. There was little or no prospect of a successful rebellion centred on dissident army officers in Syria. The nationalists urged the Hashemites to seek an agreement with the British on the basis of terms they had agreed and drawn up in the document referred to by Antonius as the 'Damascus Protocol' and to go into open revolt against the Sultan.[18] The document set out the terms under which the Arabs would form an alliance with Britain and take up arms against the Turks. It was a wide-ranging demand for independence of all the Arabic-speaking territories of the Ottoman Empire. Feisal was skeptical that it would be acceptable to the British. He also had little hope that a revolt would succeed. In spite of Feisal's doubts, this document formed the essence of Hussein's first letter in July 1915 to McMahon.[19]

Feisal continued to hedge his bets at every stage: again promising support from the Hejaz to Jemal Pasha, an ardent pan-Islamist who had been Turkish commander in Syria since December 1914, and who frequently and forcefully beseeched Hussein to declare *Jihad*. Feisal, while an advocate of revolt at some stage, was cautious about the timing. When he, his father and his brother Abdullah met for a council of war in June 1915, Feisal stated that he was anxious to see Turkey significantly weakened before the Arabs took the field. Abdullah, however, was anxious to proceed with all possible haste. He seems to have been motivated by a fear that, unless the Arabs moved quickly, they would lose any rights at the Peace Conference: *The war could have only one consequence for the Arabs: they would remain in the noose of [tyrannical] government whether the Turks and Germans or the French and British won; it was necessary to proclaim the Arab movement and [thus] escape through war the necessary consequence of submission to alien rule.*[20]

'The war could have only one consequence for the Arabs: they would remain in the noose of [tyrannical] government whether the Turks and Germans or the French and British won; it was necessary to proclaim the Arab movement and [thus] escape through war the necessary consequence of submission to alien rule.'
EMIR ABDULLAH

Abdullah was the Hashemite most committed to rebellion. This had come to the notice of the Ottoman authorities who, he claimed, tried to buy him off with offers of high office (the position of *Vali* in Yemen). He confided to T E Lawrence that, even without the war, there would have been an uprising, to be started by Hussein and his confederates taking pilgrims hostage during the *Hajj*. This action was intended to draw in the Great Powers, including Britain and France, to force a compromise, which would gain Hussein immunity from Turkish pressure in the future. This rather fanciful plan was mooted to take place in 1915 but the War had forced its postponement.[21] Hussein backed Abdullah's reasoning that now was the time to make a claim for a seat at the post-war peace conference. It was decided to offer the British an alliance in return for their acceptance of the demands in the Damascus Protocol. An unsigned letter from Hussein was sent to Henry McMahon with a letter from Abdullah to Ronald Storrs dated 14 July 1915 enclosed.

Some historians are skeptical of Hussein's sudden espousal of Arab nationalism. Mary Wilson, for instance, sees it as essentially self-serving. Hussein's main motivation was his dislike of the secularising and centralising impulses of the CUP.[22] Indeed, suspicion of the secular CUP leadership in Constantinople was a key motivating factor for many in the Hejaz. Hussein believed the Ottomans had forfeited their right to the Caliphate and he was the most suitable leader to assume the position. However, to have emphasised Islamic zealotry as the primary motivation for rising against the Ottomans might have led the British, who had the empire with the greatest Islamic population, to have had second thoughts about backing Hussein. It was much safer to wrap the Hashemite cause in the banner of Arab nationalism, which at this time presented no threat to British interests. Efraim Karsh goes further: the revolt 'was Hussein's personal bid for an empire. The Sherif was no champion of national liberation seeking to unshackle the "Arab Nation" from the chains of Ottoman captivity: he was an imperialist aspirant anxious to exploit a unique window of opportunity for substituting his own empire for that of the Ottomans.'[23] Historical opinion is united in agreement that Hussein's motivations had little to do with Arab nationalism. However, there is dispute about what Hussein's ambitions actually were. Were they to build a personal empire or to win the Caliphate? The evidence remains unclear.

3

Negotiating for an Arab State

By July 1915, the British position in the Middle East had deteriorated substantially. The Anglo-French attack on Gallipoli, aimed at dealing a knockout blow to Turkey, had clearly failed and the Expeditionary Force would withdraw by the end of the year. Hussein was now in a position to secure a premium from the British for leading a revolt against the Turks. Reflecting this, Hussein's opening gambit, his letter of 14 July 1915, was certainly a bold one. (This is the first in the sequence of letters that came to be known as the McMahon-Hussein correspondence.) He demanded that he be recognised as King of an Arab state encompassing the whole of the Arabian Peninsula (apart from Aden) as far north as Mersina and bounded by the Mediterranean, the Red Sea, the Persian Gulf and Persia. This would include all of modern-day Syria, Israel-Palestine, Jordan, Iraq, Saudi Arabia, the Gulf States and most of Yemen. He also wanted Britain to approve the proclamation of an Arabic Caliphate.[1] Unsurprisingly British officials in Cairo thought Hussein's requests unrealistic. Ronald Storrs, the Oriental Secretary, later wrote: 'It was at the time and still is my opinion that the Sherif opened his mouth and the British Government their purse a good deal too wide ... We could not conceal from ourselves (and with difficulty from him) that his pretensions bordered upon the tragi-comic.'[2]

Nonetheless, the blow to British confidence caused by the setback at Gallipoli is surely evidenced by the decision not to reject out of hand what were in many respects the out-rageous demands of a minor Arab potentate. Instead, via the High Commissioner in Egypt Sir Henry McMahon, the British government decided to engage in a lengthy sequence of correspondence (some ten letters) with Hussein.[3] The McMahon-Hussein exchange culminated in a military alli-ance between Britain and the Hashemites that was to be maintained for more than 40 years. However, the exchanges were less clear-cut and more ambiguous regarding the politi-cal agreements that were made. In essence, the questions left unresolved revolved around the degree of Arab independence and the territorial extent of this Arab state.[4] Why was this the case? Elie Kedourie argues that the British replies were 'at once deliberately vague and unwittingly obscure'.[5] McMahon believed his task was to tempt 'the Arab people onto the right path, detach them from the enemy and bring them on to our side'.[6] He perhaps crafted the correspondence more carefully than he is sometimes given credit. It was in British interests that Hussein might think that more was on the table than was really being offered, while at the same time, the vagueness of the correspondence meant that the British promises would contain so much ambiguity that no objective reader would be able to decipher what exactly had been promised. The words chosen allowed a certain degree of deniability.

McMahon's first response was sent on 30 August 1915. It was an understandably evasive reply supporting the liberation of the Arabs from Turkish rule and an Arabic Caliphate. However, McMahon felt it was premature to discuss boundary details in the heat of war, while Turkey remained in occupation, and when there were increasing signs that Hashemite influence in Syria was very weak and the Syrian Arabs were tending to align themselves with the Ottomans. Hussein replied on 9 September demanding a precise delineation of the boundaries of the putative Arab state. He wrote, ominously, that a failure to deal with the matter might be taken 'to infer an estrangement or something of the sort'.[7]

It is possible the correspondence might have ended at this point in disagreement or that the British would have taken a stronger line with Hussein. However, new developments had occurred: primarily the secret mission to Cairo by Muhammad Sherif al-Faruqi, an Arab staff officer in the Ottoman army and apparently a leading figure in the Arab nationalist group *al Ahd*. In an interview with Brigadier Clayton, Chief of Military Intelligence in Cairo, in the autumn of 1915, he revealed that Syrian Arab nationalist societies would take up arms on the side of the British. In return for this they wanted explicit British support for an independent Arab state. If they did not get such an assurance, they would provide full support for Turkey and Germany in the war.[8] It is now generally accepted that al-Faruqi exaggerated the strength of Arab nationalism and his contacts with the Turks and Germans. There is no evidence that the Turks had any interest in appeasing Arab nationalism and the Germans would not lightly have undertaken negotiations behind the back of their ally. Nonetheless, the interview and the reports that were drawn from it appear to have led British officials and soldiers in Cairo to conclude that a deal acceptable to Sherif Hussein must be put on the table as soon as possible. Lord Kitchener in London was strongly supportive of keeping the Arabs on side. 'You must do your best to prevent any alienation of the Arabs' traditional loyalty to England,' he stated unambiguously.[9] He may well have believed that an Arab rebellion in Syria led by dissident army units might still save the Gallipoli campaign, which was teetering on the edge of collapse.[10]

McMahon was given considerable leeway in drafting a reply by Sir Edward Grey, the Foreign Secretary, who was reasonably well disposed to a strategy of wooing the Arabs. Grey, nonetheless, feared that promising too much to the Arabs might cause friction with the French, who would probably perceive Hussein to be a British proxy. McMahon, without fully consulting all the relevant Whitehall departments, especially India Office colleagues who were aghast when they learnt of what had been offered, dispatched his letter to Hussein on 24 October 1915. Its exact meaning has become a source of great controversy in the Middle East, as well as being the basis of a substantial cottage industry for historians.[11] Because of its importance, the key passages of the letter from McMahon to Hussein of 24 October 1915 are printed in the panel on page 48.

What exactly did the British exclusions mean? The lack of a map appended to the letter left certain issues open to interpretation. Was Palestine included in the exceptions that the British had made? How much of Syria was excluded? By the end of 1915 the sole point of contention between McMahon and Hussein was over certain territories in Syria, namely the *vilayets* of Aleppo and Beirut, which the French had made clear they wished to have for themselves after the War. Hussein wrote to McMahon on 16 January 1916 informing him that these areas had to form part of the Arab kingdom. However, he understood the need for harmonious relations

MCMAHON TO HUSSEIN, LETTER OF 24 OCTOBER 1915

'The two districts of Mesina and Alexandretta and portions of Syria lying to the west of the districts of Damascus, Horns and Aleppo cannot be said to be purely Arab, and should be excluded from the limits demanded [by the Arabs].

With the above modification, and without prejudice to our existing treaties with Arab chiefs, we accept those limits.

As for those regions lying within these frontiers wherein Great Britain is free to act without detriment to the interests of her ally, France, I am empowered in the name of the government of Great Britain to give the following assurances and make the following reply to your letter.

1) Subject to the above modifications, Great Britain is prepared to recognise and support the independence of the Arabs in the regions within the limits demanded by the Sherif of Mecca.

2) Great Britain will guarantee the Holy Places against all external aggression and will recognise their inviolability.

3) When the situation admits, Great Britain will give to the Arabs her advice and will assist them to establish what may appear to be the most suitable forms of government in those various territories.

4) On the other hand, it is understood that the Arabs have decided to seek the advice and guidance of Great Britain only, and that such European advisors and officials as may be required for the formation of a sound administration will be British.

5) With regards to the *vilayets* of Baghdad and Basra, the Arabs will recognise that the established position and interests of Great Britain necessitate special administrative arrangements in order to secure these territories from foreign aggression to promote the welfare of the local populations and to safeguard our mutual economic interests.'

between Britain and France and would not press the matter until the conclusion of hostilities. To summarise, the British had managed to exclude considerable areas that Hussein desired in return for the uprising of the Arabs against the Ottomans and their support of the Entente.

Towards the Arab Revolt

Hussein, however, appears to have been dissatisfied with the British response and continued to prevaricate over whether to launch his revolt. Jemal, the Turkish commander in Syria, placed him under increasing pressure to provide a military contingent from the Hejaz and Feisal had to be sent to meet him. At the same time, the Turks were beginning to crack down on Arab nationalist groups in Syria and within the army. Feisal now believed only nationalists of the second rank were available to revolt. Hussein continued to play a double game. He accepted McMahon's offer and the British began to ship gold and weaponry to him in the spring of 1916, but he also continued to maintain relations with the Ottoman government. Feisal sought from Jemal an assurance that, should Hussein raise a force to aid the Ottomans, he would then be given full autonomy without a Turkish governor. Jemal would give no such assurance.

Enver put further pressure on Hussein in the spring of 1916. Hussein replied with a shopping list of demands. There would be no volunteers and no declaration of *Jihad* until Arab demands were met. These included the release of Arab political prisoners, autonomy for the Arab part of the Empire, and the recognition of the Hashemite Emirate as hereditary. Hussein was now getting very close to treason. Enver firmly rejected Hussein's demands for the release of prisoners and Jemal warned him that his position was at risk if the Turks won the war. Enver and Jemal sensed an imminent break with Hussein and Turkish forces began to prepare to meet an Arab revolt. Eyeing these preparations, Hussein decided that he had to take the initiative. His sons, Feisal, Abdullah and Ali, were directed to organise the Hejaz for revolt. Final messages were sent to Constantinople demanding that the Arab demands be met. When no response was received, the Arab Revolt began on 5 June 1916 with a proclamation in Mecca by Hussein and a series of simultaneous attacks on Turkish forces and infrastructure across the Hejaz.[12]

The Sykes-Picot Agreement

The literary power of T E Lawrence's *Seven Pillars of Wisdom* and the sweeping cinematic grandeur of David Lean's 1962 epic, *Lawrence of Arabia*, have hugely coloured the Western popular view of the Arab Revolt. Moreover, George Antonius's *The Arab Awakening* helped mould Arab perceptions of the Revolt and the alleged duplicity of Britain. The pages of the major academic journals on the Middle East and modern history, as well as countless books, have been filled with articles criticising and denouncing the Hashemites, the British and the French and their respective academic detractors and supporters since Sylvia Haim and Elie Kedourie first took up cudgels against Antonius in the early 1950s. The two most substantial elements in the Arab claim of duplicity against the British were the top-secret Sykes-Picot Agreement of 1916 (published by the Bolsheviks in late 1917 in the aftermath of the October Revolution) and the Balfour Declaration of November 1917. Both documents, according to their critics, were the complete antithesis of the McMahon-Hussein correspondence. In particular, the Sykes-Picot Agreement was deeply controversial and it is to this we should now turn.

Sir Mark Sykes,[13] a baronet and a Conservative MP, was a rich and remarkably well-travelled expert on the Ottoman Empire and the Middle East. After failing to complete his studies at Cambridge, he spent many years travelling in the Ottoman Empire and the Middle East including some four years in the British Embassy at Constantinople. After his election as a Conservative MP in 1911, he became his party's expert on the Ottoman Empire. Thanks to friendships with those around Kitchener, he gained employment in the War Office before becoming that Department's representative on the de Bunsen Committee, where his knowledge of Ottoman affairs allowed him to influence the deliberations of the Committee. Soon after, he was dispatched on a six-month fact-finding mission to the Balkans and the Middle East. Sykes rapidly became aware of a serious split between Britain's two major centres of power in the region. The British administration in Cairo was extremely anxious to pursue the Arab nationalist option, while in India, there was serious thought being given to a scheme to settle large numbers of Indians in southern Mesopotamia should Britain conquer that area.

Sykes was a charming and outgoing sort by many accounts, though he held many obnoxious views. He seems to have had an almost obsessive fear of Jews and was given to disparaging many of the various nationalities of the Ottoman Middle East including the Armenians and the Arabs. However, he began to see these nationalities he once disparaged as the key to a swift victory for the British in the Middle East. This belief made Sykes an enthusiastic advocate of an Arab revolt and he may well have played some role in making McMahon more amenable to accepting many of Hussein's demands in the autumn of 1915. His new enthusiasm for the Arab cause and his concerns about the disparity in attitudes and views between London, Cairo and India led him to advocate the creation of an Arab Bureau that would co-ordinate British policy in the Middle East. This came into operation in early 1916.

On his return to London, after putting forward his views

for greater co-ordination of British Middle Eastern policy, Sykes ended up taking the lead in Britain's negotiations with France regarding the partition of the Ottoman Empire. The McMahon-Hussein correspondence was the catalyst for these talks beginning in earnest. Sir Edward Grey, the Foreign Secretary, was concerned that rumours about these negotiations would reach the French. They might consider the wooing of the Arabs to be a British attempt to use Hussein as a proxy to keep the French out of Syria. Grey, unlike Kitchener and the Cairo authorities, did not see France as a potential future enemy and he may well have viewed an amicable agreement on the Ottoman Empire as a means of cementing the Anglo-French Entente.[14] Immediately after McMahon's October 1915 message to Hussein, Grey informed Paul Cambon, the French Ambassador to the United Kingdom, of Britain's contacts with Arab nationalists and suggested the desirability of sorting out Anglo-French thinking on the Ottoman Middle East at the earliest juncture.

Cambon appointed his trusted First Secretary Georges Picot as the French negotiator. He was a strong supporter of French colonial ambitions.[15] The French were distrustful of the British involvement with the Arabs and did not like the idea of an Arab Kingdom. Picot was instructed to ensure that France's area of control and/or influence should be greatly expanded to the north in Cilicia, to the east to encompass Mosul and to the south to include Palestine. France's ambitions were to extend as much as possible the territory that it would directly control and to ensure that it enjoyed virtually untrammeled power within its area or sphere of influence within the Arab Kingdom. This Kingdom was envisaged, by the Quai d'Orsay as a weak, loose federation or confederation that would have virtually no serious powers. French advisors would consequently exercise a controlling influence via local princes and emirs.[16]

Picot began negotiations on 23 November 1915 with a seven-member interdepartmental committee chaired by the Foreign Office's Permanent Undersecretary, Sir Arthur Nicolson, who had long been a strong advocate of the closest cooperation between the Entente Powers. The British, however were surprised by the extent of France's demands – though these were probably an opening gambit. As Picot himself commented: 'Our task is to make our demands and [then] to abandon ground only foot by foot if compelled to do so; that way we shall always have some ground left.'[17] The initial round of talks failed to produce an agreement. Sykes, then, became the War Office's representative on the committee. He successfully proposed to Picot and the committee that he should negotiate solely with Picot during the second round of talks. It is not entirely clear why this was the case. Sykes was known to have Francophile tendencies and to be broadly sympathetic to French Catholic interests in the Levant, particularly in the Lebanon and Syria. On the other hand he was considered by some to be a mouthpiece for Kitchener and his broadly anti-French views. Also, he had already explained to al-Faruqi, in Cairo in October 1915, the necessity for the Arabs to accept a large degree of French interference and control over an Arab state that contained Syria, Palestine, and Lebanon. France, Sykes made clear, would have a monopoly over the supply of all the political advisers and retain control over educational institutions, railways and any new economic enterprises in their sphere of influence.[18]

By the end of January 1916, Sykes and Picot had hammered out an agreement. It was decided that Britain would annex the Tigris-Euphrates valley from the Arabian Gulf to Baghdad.

Additionally, Britain would have indirect control (i.e. priority in economic and political rights) in the area between the lines Akaba–Kuwait and Haifa–Tekrit, while France would have similar rights in the area delimited by the lines Haifa–Tekrit and the southern edge of Kurdistan. France's areas of direct control would be the modern day Lebanon, coastal Syria and a considerable portion of Central Anatolia. The British, it appears were content to see the French extend their sphere to buffer the British sphere against Russia, which it was assumed would be the dominant power in most of Asiatic Turkey. Palestine, apart from some strategic British bases, would be subject to international control. Outside of Palestine and the areas of direct control, an Arab state or group of states would be allowed. However, this Arab state's independence would be circumscribed by the fact that it would be split into British and French spheres of influence. What the British and French were envisaging was that the method by which they exercised control over Egypt and Morocco – where local governments existed but were dominated by British and French officials respectively – would be exported to the Middle East.

Sykes and Picot signed the Agreement on 31 January 1916, and after some modifications, the governments of Britain and France endorsed it in February. However, it was to only come into effect if Russia agreed and the Arabs rebelled. The first condition was fulfilled in May 1916 and the Arab Revolt began a month later. If Hussein had been aware of the Agreement at the time, there is little doubt he would have found it extremely troubling though hardly surprising. He would probably have been more concerned about what the British and French really thought about the future prospects of an Arab state. Picot considered that the British had offered a lot to the Arabs but his and the French Foreign Office's view was that an Arab state would not last beyond the end of the War. Sir Arthur Nicolson shared this view, believing that Hussein's Arab Kingdom was absurd and impractical.[19]

Historians and the Sykes-Picot Agreement[20]

George Antonius's *The Arab Awakening* is perhaps the most influential denunciation of the Sykes-Picot Agreement and the Balfour Declaration of 1917, which promised to establish a national home for Jews in Palestine. Antonius's claims of great betrayal lie in four main discrepancies between what the British promised Hussein and the Sykes-Picot Agreement and the Balfour Declaration. The first of these discrepancies were the portions of Syria lying to the west of the districts of Damascus, Homs, Hama and Aleppo. McMahon made clear that the areas excluded were those that 'cannot be said to be purely Arab'. Antonius's view was that this only excluded some areas of the Lebanon and Turkish-populated Alexandretta. Nonetheless, all of this area was to be handed over to direct French control under the Sykes-Picot agreement. Secondly, Palestine was first given over to international control and then promised as a national home to the Jews despite not being explicitly excluded from the area to be allocated to an Arab state by McMahon. Thirdly, the limitations placed on independence of the interior of Syria were not explicit in the McMahon correspondence. Fourthly and finally, the British areas for direct control of the area from Baghdad to the Persian Gulf, i.e. what is now southern Iraq, were not excluded by McMahon.[21] What might be called the Elie Kedourie School forcefully rejected these points and suggested that Britain's dealings with the Hashemites were above board. Kedourie was especially certain that there was no incompatibility in the promises in the McMahon correspondence with Hussein and the Sykes-Picot Agreement, and moreover, in 1916 and 1917 Hussein was informed about it both directly and indirectly by the Allies and understood what it meant.[22] However, Kedourie did admit that the means by which the terms of the Agreement were relayed to Hussein were uncertain.[23]

The answer as to who is correct lies somewhere between the Arab and British interpretations. In return for promises of a widespread Arab revolt that he only partially delivered, Hussein, a relatively minor Arab emir with extremely limited military means, succeeded in getting the Entente Powers to recognise an enormous Arab Kingdom substantially bigger than Britain and France combined. It was inevitable that the independence of such an entity was going to be circumscribed though perhaps not as much as it was under the Mandate system that eventually emerged in the post-war period. What was unacceptable in international relations later, secret deals and the carving-up of territories, was the done thing in the era of pre-Paris Peace Conference diplomacy. The Anglo-French and Anglo-Russian Ententes, for instance, had emerged in the first decade of the 20th century from a series of colonial carve-ups and understandings.

It was also inevitable that the fringes of this Arab state or federation were going to be chipped away at. It is certainly true that the British did not explicitly exclude Palestine from the McMahon-Hussein correspondence. It is possible that Cairo exceeded its instructions in not specifically excluding it. However, if the British, especially in London, had considered the matter more carefully, they would have done so. Malcolm Yapp suggests that Cairo may have kept the question of boundaries open. If a weak Arab confederation, dominated by the British, ended up as the successor state of the Ottoman

Empire, it did not really matter what its boundaries were.[24] Even better, it would leave the French with less territory.

Critics of the British government such as Antonius and Western academics such as Arnold Toynbee were simply holding Britain to too high a standard of behaviour. Was Britain obliged to meet every single Arab demand? Where there was ambiguity was it not always likely, if not certain, that the might of the British army on the ground in the Middle East was going to prevail over Hashemite interpretations of correspondence? During wars (and at many other times) states lie or promise more than they can or are willing to deliver. Hussein would have to have been very credulous to believe that at the final peace conference all his territorial demands would be met. As Harold Temperley notes: 'The secret Agreements relating to the Near and Middle East to which various Allies subscribed during the war [should be placed] in their proper perspective ... the gigantic struggle for national survival, which required of the nations involved in it the use of every expedient permissible in diplomacy and war.'[25]

> 'The secret Agreements relating to the Near and Middle East to which various Allies subscribed during the war (should be placed) in their proper perspective ... the gigantic struggle for national survival, which required of the nations involved in it the use of every expedient permissible in diplomacy and war.'
> HAROLD TEMPERLEY

On the other hand, Kedourie and Isaiah Friedman's attempts to show that the British were always clear that Palestine was excluded also depend on putting the best possible face on the available evidence. They also seem to perceive a morality in British policy at the height of the greatest war that had been fought up to then that is perhaps more apparent to them than to others. They seem to suggest that the British did not lie or mislead in their dealings.

Lloyd George, writing 20 years later, was highly critical of the Sykes-Picot Agreement, particularly the failure to consult Hussein. 'Why the British Government did not notify them of this important agreement is incomprehensible. They were directly concerned for it disposed of their future government in wide areas of great renown. When it became known to the Arab leaders, it naturally gave offence to them.'[26]

It is argued that Hussein was informed of the Agreement (see Chapter 4) but this again seems to have been communicated to him in a vague manner. Hussein remained convinced till the day he died that the British had misled him. He was sure that on both the issues of territory and the extent of the independence of the Arab state, he was correct in his interpretation. Historical opinion is generally against his viewpoint but nonetheless the story of betrayal that he propagated through George Antonius is widely accepted in the Middle East. Many British policymakers, as Elie Kedourie has pointed out, shared the view that a wrong had been inflicted on the Arabs.[27]

Perhaps the major fault and underlying unpleasantness of British and French behaviour, especially in the Sykes-Picot Agreement, is not the betrayal of the Arabs' territorial ambitions – for which every piece of evidence supporting Arab claims is countered by enough ambiguities to render claims such as those to the littoral of Syria or Palestine meaningless – but the assumption on the part of the British and French governments that those parts that the Arabs were to receive would be nothing more than puppet states. However, it can be argued that the Arab states envisaged could not possibly have stood on their own feet for a considerable period of time after Ottoman rule ended. There was bound to be a period when they would need aid and advice from outside powers.[28] Otherwise, there was a high likelihood that they would break up along ethic, religious and tribal lines.

4
The Arab Revolt

Difficulties in the Revolt

Hussein's raising of the standard of revolt on 5 June 1916 turned out to be rather a damp squib. Both he and the Arab Bureau had greatly exaggerated the likely extent of the revolt. For example, in his letter to McMahon of 16 February 1916, Hussein implied that 100,000 Arab soldiers in the Ottoman army would defect to his revolt. The Arab Bureau strongly backed this supposition as well. However, it never happened. The vast majority of Arab troops remained scrupulously loyal to the Ottoman Empire.[1] It would appear that the Arab Bedouin forces, virtually all irregulars, that Hussein was able to field never exceeded 15,000 men. Moreover, the geographical extent of the Arab Revolt was limited as well. No rising took place in Syria or Palestine due to Jemal's preemptive action in crushing potential dissidents among the Arabs in the army. Indeed, to keep the rebellion going, Britain had to lavish large amounts of money and arms on the Arabs. Direct British military involvement was limited mainly to the provision of advisers and occasional naval and air support.

The limited nature of Hussein's revolt was a disappointment

to the British though they were glad to see a revolt had at least occurred. After an initial success with the capture of Mecca, the Arab forces made little progress. Utterly lacking in any tactical ability and fearful of exposing themselves to Ottoman artillery, their only other initial success was the capture of the Red Sea port of Jeddah and that was only because the British provided naval and air support. Taif did not fall until September 1916, while Turkish forces held Medina until early in 1919, months after the conclusion of hostilities. By mid-July 1916, the revolt was running out of steam. Hussein found it difficult to maintain a disciplined force in the field and desertion was rife. Feisal, the most militarily astute and the bravest of Hussein's sons, confided to Colonel Cyril Wilson in August 1916 that the Turks would prevail if they took the offensive. Soon afterwards Feisal requested British landings on the coast of the Hejaz to aid the revolt.[2] Hussein was apparently undisturbed by his growing military problems, proclaiming himself King of the Arabs in October 1916. However, the British had become deeply concerned and at the end of 1916 it was decided to step up aid to Hussein. His subsidy was increased from £125,000 to £200,000 a month. Large quantities of rifles were also supplied – far in excess of Hussein's requirements. The subsidy was vital for the Revolt since gold, rather than appeals to patriotism, was the key to recruiting Bedouin tribesmen. However, haggling over the price often hindered the timely execution of military operations as did the general lack of discipline of the Bedouins. Battles would be broken off due to fallings-out between apparently allied tribesmen and on one memorable occasion even to stop for coffee. T E Lawrence, who became the Arabs' key military adviser from the end of 1916, was often critical of the tendency of Bedouin forces to go home with plunder before achieving their objective.[3] The strategic direction of the Revolt was increasingly removed from Hussein's hands. Colonel C E Wilson, commanding the British military mission to the Hejaz, and General Gilbert Clayton, the head of military intelligence in Cairo, took increasingly influential roles, Clayton coordinating much of British support for the Arab Revolt through the Arab Bureau.[4]

The Arab Bureau

William Reginald ('Blinker') Hall, Director of the Intelligence Division, recruited David Hogarth, an eminent British archaeologist of the Near and Middle East, to join a group of British officers and officials who would co-ordinate British dealings with the Arabs – this would become the Arab Bureau. Hogarth subsequently recruited one of his protégés, T E Lawrence, and an Arabist, Gertrude Bell. Cairo became the base of the Arab Bureau from March 1916. Gilbert Clayton headed up the bureau and Ronald Storrs had a role as well. The Arab Bureau provided information, reports and policy briefings on Syria, Arabia and Palestine for the British government. Its most notable publication was the *Arab Bulletin*, a confidential briefing book, which was circulated to senior British officials from spring 1916.

The Bureau is also usually characterised as extremely francophobic. Clayton, Hogarth, Lawrence, Bell and the new British High Commissioner to Egypt, Reginald Wingate, certainly exhibited antipathy towards French aims in the Middle East. They viewed the Hashemites as a potential means of reducing or eliminating French influence in Syria. Some historians have tended to view the Arab Bureau as a group of innocents and enthusiasts entirely taken in by the Arab cause and the Hashemites. They, it is claimed, were determined to see their protégés and their cause achieve at least some of its post-war goals at the expense of the French. Some historians reason that the cause of this was its members' guilt over the contradictions between the Sykes-Picot Agreement and the Hussein-McMahon correspondence. What the Arab Bureau was most interested in, however, was the expansion of British imperial interests in the Arab world. They saw a loose confederation nominally under Hussein but informally controlled by Britain as the best means of achieving this.[5] They also saw this as a means of reducing, if not eliminating, French influence in the Arab World. T E Lawrence, in an oft-quoted passage written after the war, suggested the possibility of formal constitutional links between Britain and the successor Arab state of the Ottoman Empire: 'My own ambition is that the Arabs should be our first brown dominion, and not our last brown colony.'[6]

The emergence of T E Lawrence

Perhaps the most important figure in the Arab Bureau was a young subaltern, T E Lawrence. Both man of action and intellectual, his role in the Arab Bureau was due primarily to a knowledge of the Middle East gained during his extensive travels there before the First World War. He had developed an enthusiasm for traditional Arab culture as well as a hostility towards modernisers, be they Young Turks or French missionaries and educators. Unsurprisingly, the anti-French views of the Arab Bureau influenced him as well. After a mission in early 1916 to Mesopotamia, where he witnessed the incompetent British campaign, he was ordered to Jeddah with Ronald Storrs in October 1916, with a brief to appraise the Arab Revolt. He would spend the next two years in Arabia playing a leading role in it. Lawrence certainly had

T E Lawrence[7] (1888–1935), intelligence officer and writer. The illegitimate son of an Anglo-Irish landowner, the Oxford educated Lawrence spent considerable time between 1909 and 1914 on various archaeological digs in the Levant. Due to his knowledge of the Middle East, he was sent to Cairo in 1914 where he was primarily desk-bound until arriving in the Hejaz in October 1916. There he rapidly assumed a key role in the Arab Revolt, building it around Feisal, Hussein's most dynamic son. He accompanied the Arab delegation under Feisal to the Peace Conference. His experiences would provide the source material for *Seven Pillars of Wisdom*, his epic but controversial retelling of the campaign in the desert. He left government service in August 1919 to become a Fellow of All Souls, Oxford. He was recalled by Winston Churchill to serve as Middle East adviser in 1921–2 where he had a key role in implementing the so-called 'Sherifian Solution', which involved the establishment of Hashemite rule in Iraq and Transjordan. He later joined the RAF under the pseudonym Archibald Ross. Soon after leaving the service, he was tragically killed in a motorcycle accident. His legend was further enhanced by David Lean's film *Lawrence of Arabia* (1962). Since the publication of Richard Aldington's hostile biography[8] in the 1950s, questions about his reliability as witness to the events described in his writings have regularly surfaced nearly as much as claims and revelations about his private life and sexuality.

a major impact on the Revolt, which was struggling desperately by the time he arrived. It was clear by October 1916 that the Turks held the military initiative. There was no prospect of the Arabs being able to take Medina. Furthermore, there was no sign that Hussein was attracting support outside the narrow confines of the Bedouin tribes and what support was forthcoming was entirely due to bribes funded from the British subsidy.

Lawrence quickly concluded that the Revolt needed to focus around the most dynamic of Hussein's sons, Feisal: 'I felt at first glance that this was the man I had come to Arabia to seek – the leader who would bring the Arab Revolt to full glory,' he wrote later.[9] Lawrence recognised that Feisal was not without faults – he viewed him as excessively tribal in his allegiances. The alternatives, his three brothers, were far worse: Ali suffered from ill health, Zeid was too young and callow, and Abdullah, the most obvious choice, was considered by Lawrence to be too much of a politician and not enough of a statesman.[10] In any case, Lawrence considered him militarily incompetent. He was able to persuade the head of the Arab Bureau, Gilbert Clayton, of the merits of this despite some reluctance on his part. Feisal was not a universally popular choice for leadership among the Arab Bureau. Abdullah had been the most enthusiastic about launching the Revolt and moreover, had initiated the contacts with the British. Feisal, on the other hand, had been the most reluctant to rebel. However, as the Revolt had developed his attitude towards the Ottomans had hardened and while he remained open to the possibility of rapprochement (see below), he considered it increasingly unlikely that any acceptable deal could be reached.[11]

> 'I felt at first glance that this was the man I had come to Arabia to seek – the leader who would bring the Arab Revolt to full glory.'
>
> T E LAWRENCE ON FEISAL

Clayton became increasingly dependent on Lawrence for information on the Arab Revolt and operations in the Northern Hejaz. Lawrence went from being a minor figure to a major influence due to his ability to control the information that was reaching Cairo. From November 1916, he became liaison officer to the Arab Revolt. This gave him a central role in deciding on Feisal's strategy. His control and supervision of the British subsidy and arms deliveries gave him real power. However, his brilliance was in his ability to forge a working partnership with Feisal and other Arabs by adapting himself successfully to the sensitivities of Arab culture. His tact and diplomacy helped smooth over some of the serious problems that faced the Anglo-Hashemite alliance.

There seems to be little doubt that Lawrence's arrival proved to be a major spur to the Arab Revolt. His key tactical decision was to utilise the Arabs' great advantage: their mobility thanks to their skills with camels and horses. Their great disadvantage was their vulnerability to casualties, which could not be afforded as Arab morale was extremely fragile. It was better, Lawrence recognised, to use the open spaces of the desert to avoid a war of contact but instead fight one of detachment.[12] Attacks would only be pressed home when the Arabs had the tactical advantage. Lawrence, therefore, aligned Arab tactics and strategy with their military resources and capabilities as well the geography of the Hejaz. In his view, attacks should be generally confined to soft targets such as railway lines, infrastructure and supply convoys rather than frontal assaults on Turkish infantry, which tended to end in disaster. He saw little point in pressing home attacks on major Turkish concentrations such as at Medina. The inability of the Arabs to stand up to artillery bombardment precluded this. It was much better to leave the 25,000-strong garrison bottled up, where it remained impotent for the course of the war.[13] Instead, little pinprick attacks, similar to the raids that were a frequent occurrence in the early 20th century Arabian Peninsula during peacetime, would keep the Arabs in the field and build up their confidence. He also allowed the Arabs to keep plunder from their attacks. It was simply pointless to enforce Western military discipline on nomadic Bedouins when they could simply up and leave if they were not happy with their conditions. In key engagements, including the capture of Akaba in July 1917, Lawrence demonstrated considerable tactical flair and the ability to exploit a military situation.

Feisal takes command

Feisal was transformed from being one of a number of brothers to *primus inter pares*. Feisal would now eclipse his elder brother Abdullah and ultimately even his father. He became the driving Arab force behind the Revolt. Having spent much of his childhood in Constantinople, he and his brothers were not natural Bedouin. Indeed many Arabs would have considered them *effendi*, an Arabic term to describe Arabs of noble rank who had received a modern secular education and had adopted Western clothing and concepts. As soon as they returned to Mecca, their father had insisted that they act like Bedouin. They were sent out into the wilderness without comforts to get back to their roots. However, their upbringing isolated them from their fellow Bedouin. As Lawrence noted, the four sons of Hussein 'were natives of no country, lovers of no private plot of ground. They had no real confidants or ministers; and no one of them seemed open to another, or to the father, of whom they stood in awe.' [14]

Robert Lansing, the American Secretary of State, left behind a memorable description of Feisal when he was at the Paris Peace Conference:

'The features of the Arab Prince were clear-cut, regular, and typical of his race.... His complexion was sallow and slightly mottled like the majority of those of pure Semitic blood. His face was thin and, though with few lines and wrinkles, was strong and earnest in expression. His dark eyes were serene and kindly, but one could easily imagine that they would flash fire under the excitement of conflict or the impulse of violent emotion. Candor and truth were in the straight forward look from his eyes.... One felt his reserve power and his strength of character, while there was the feeling that he possessed a profundity of thought which raised him above the common man.' [15]

Lawrence and Feisal's relationship was the key to the successes that the Arab Revolt enjoyed. Feisal always gave the orders, while Lawrence merely advised. It was simply unrealistic for Lawrence to give orders to Feisal. He had to persuade him and then let Feisal direct his men. Both Feisal and his father were at times extremely difficult to deal with. Nonetheless, Lawrence and Feisal forged a useful partnership.

Part of the reason for the closeness was that Lawrence was willing to confide some of the most secret aspects of British policy to Feisal. In February 1917, he explained to him that the McMahon correspondence had been superseded by the Sykes-Picot Agreement and France was going to have a major role in the post-war settlement in the region. Moving north and spreading the Revolt into Syria was the only way of forestalling French claims there. Lawrence's revelations appear to have been motivated by proposals of the small French military mission in the Hejaz to stage an attack on the port of Akaba. Lawrence persuaded Feisal that this was meant to bottle the Arabs up in the Hejaz and leave the French a free hand in Syria. Feisal now knew how it was vitally important for him to move north and take Damascus and the main Syrian cities.[16]

The first sign that the tactics Lawrence advocated would work was seen in the attack on the coastal town of Wejh, which was far to the north of Jeddah and Mecca and would provide a base from which operations against the Hejaz railway could be carried out. It also pointed to the extension of operations out of the Hejaz and into Syria itself. Supported by British naval forces, the town fell to Feisal's men on 23 January 1917. From here, the Arabs were able to conduct their hit-and-run operations against the Hejaz railway. The Ottomans, forced to divert ever more resources into keeping the railway open, stood on the defensive for the rest of the campaign. They were, as Lawrence had desired, bottled up in Medina.

Lawrence disappeared from view for much of the spring and early summer of 1917. He went far into Syria in an attempt to ascertain for himself the extent of support from tribal groupings for the Arab Revolt. This appears linked to his desire to drive Feisal northwards. Upon his return to the Hejaz in June 1917, he directed an operation against the port of Akaba. The capture of Akaba convinced the British commander in the Middle East, General Sir Edmund Allenby, of the talent of Lawrence and the usefulness of the Arab Revolt. He saw Lawrence's guerrilla attacks as a means of tying-down large numbers of Ottoman troops at relatively little cost to the British. For the next year, from their base at Akaba, Lawrence and Feisal led operations against Turkish forces in the towns of Maan and Amman and the Damascus-Medina railway line, though he was never able to completely sever that link and the Ottoman garrison at Medina remained intact until well after the armistice. When Allenby and the British forces began their advance into Syria in the summer and autumn of 1918, the Arab irregular army provided a useful distraction on the flanks of the advance, though its impact tended to be exaggerated by Lawrence and the Arab leadership.[17]

Lloyd George, the Middle East and the Balfour Declaration

1917 and 1918 witnessed important political developments as well. The British government changed. David Lloyd George became Prime Minister at the end of 1916. He transformed British policy in the Middle East. It also became clear to many Arabs that British help in their struggle was costing them dearly, particularly when the Balfour Declaration and the Sykes-Picot Agreement became public knowledge at the end of 1917.

By the end of 1916, the Conservative ministers in the

coalition government had become thoroughly disillusioned with Asquith, believing he was no longer capable of running the War effectively. On 3 December 1916, they resolved to resign *en masse* unless Asquith resigned. It soon emerged that Asquith did not have the support of a good deal of his own party either. Many favoured David Lloyd George as the best candidate to win the war and he became Prime Minister on 7 December 1916. He immediately carried out radical surgery on his Cabinet. The Conservatives now took a far greater share of seats. Tellingly, the former Conservative Prime Minister Arthur Balfour replaced Grey at the Foreign Office.

Lloyd George had been the great radical of the Liberal party and most notably a fierce opponent of the Second Boer War (1899–1902). By the time he came to office in 1916, he was much more imperially minded thanks to the influence of Alfred Milner and his private secretary, Phillip Kerr (later Lord Lothian). Milner, who became Minister without Portfolio in the new Government, was a strong advocate of imperialism, having been closely involved in the administration of Egypt 1889–92, where he developed his view that it was Britain's imperial duty to save less advanced states from themselves. Lloyd George, from relatively early on in the War, had become extremely dubious about the strategy of frontal assaults on the Western Front. Instead, he was in favour of strengthening the British commitment in the Middle East as part of a strategy aimed at knocking out Germany's allies in the Eastern Mediterranean – primarily Turkey. Indeed, the Middle East was to prove to be one of the few bright spots for the Allies in 1917. While the Arab Revolt remained relatively limited in scale and scope, the Mesopotamian front saw results as Turkey found it increasingly difficult to replace its heavy losses in the Caucasus and Gallipoli. Lloyd George saw that the Middle East had the potential to offer cheap victories in contrast to the bloody stalemate in Flanders. In March 1917 after two years of struggle and many setbacks, the British finally captured Baghdad. Subsequently, the British War Cabinet established the Mesopotamia Administration Committee, which operated until July 1917. Its job was to coordinate the views of the departments with interests in Mesopotamia and plan for its future administration. Chaired by Lord Curzon, Lord President of the Council and member of the War Cabinet, with Lord Milner a member, it attempted, not altogether successfully, to work out a scheme for ruling Mesopotamia.[18]

Meanwhile leading figures in the British government spent a significant part of the summer and autumn of 1917 considering a radical proposal to endorse the cause of Zionism and back the creation of a national home for the Jews in Palestine. The Foreign Secretary Arthur Balfour was friendly with Chaim Weizmann, a Russian-born Jewish chemist, who had persuaded him of the merits of the Zionist cause as long ago as 1906. Later, Weizmann was introduced via C P Scott, the editor of the *Manchester Guardian*, to Lloyd George who was intrigued by the proposal. Herbert Samuel, a Jewish cabinet minister, also fervently endorsed the idea. While Asquith remained Prime Minister, there had been a reluctance to take on another commitment such as this. Now, with Lloyd George as Prime Minister and Balfour as Foreign Secretary, the Zionist issue was reconsidered. They were both broadly supportive. The prospects for a British endorsement of Zionism were further aided when Mark Sykes and Georges Picot revisited and revised their agreement. By June 1917, the French government had, tacitly at least, agreed that Palestine would move from international control to British control and that there was no objection to Jewish settlement there under British rule.[19] Squaring the British Cabinet took somewhat longer. The senior Jewish minister in the Cabinet, Edwin Montagu, the Secretary of State for India, was strongly opposed to the creation of a Jewish ghetto in the Middle East, which might impact on the position of assimilated Jews in Europe. Then, in October 1917, the American President Woodrow Wilson endorsed the proposal, demonstrating to Lloyd George the power of the Zionist lobby in the United States.[20] On 31 October 1917, the War Cabinet, after amending the text to provide more protection for the Palestinian Arabs, agreed the issuing of what became known as the Balfour Declaration.

It is not proposed to give a detailed account here of the origins of the Declaration. However, in summary, the conclusion of many of those who have made a detailed study of the declaration is that it was not motivated primarily by sympathy for Zionism but by *realpolitik* notions that the Declaration would aid British imperial ambitions in the Middle East.[21] Essentially, endorsing a Jewish homeland would allow Britain to become the dominant force in Palestine at the expense of the French. In Lloyd George's view, Zionists and Zionism would be a force for expanding the British Empire in the Middle East. The major point against this interpretation is of course that the British spent the next 30 years trying to wangle their way out of the commitment in the Declaration. Some more recent scholarship has suggested that the origins of the Balfour Declaration can instead be found in the British Establishment's deep-seated anti-Semitism. Lloyd George and other influential cabinet ministers as well as officials such as Mark Sykes were of the view that Jews controlled the wheels of history through their control of high finance and world revolution. Therefore, they needed to be appeased by an explicit endorsement of Zionism.[22]

In June 1917, Allenby was made commander of British forces in Egypt. Lloyd George told him he wanted Jerusalem captured by Christmas to improve morale on the home front. Allenby, however, was starved of the necessary resources and troops to take the offensive by General Sir William Robertson, the Chief of the Imperial General Staff. Only Lloyd George and the War Cabinet's insistence forced the cautious Allenby to move over to the offensive at the end of October and Jerusalem was secured in early December 1917.

Hussein and the Balfour Declaration

The public announcement of the Balfour Declaration brought no response from Sherif Hussein. While many Syrian notables loudly complained about the Declaration, Hussein remained conspicuously silent. Indeed he ordered his sons to calm the apprehensions of their followers about British intentions.[23] When Hogarth, the head of the Arab Bureau called on the King on 4 January 1918, Kedourie reports that Hussein 'enthusiastically assented' to Zionist settlement in Palestine and was '[unconcerned] over the Balfour Declaration and Zionist aims'.[24] This seems curious. Hussein had continued to argue that Palestine was part of the area to be made independent. Moreover, Hogarth's mission to Hussein appears to have deliberately downplayed the declaration and emphasised that the commitments that the British had made to Zionism had to be 'compatible with the freedom of the existing [Arab] population both economic and political...'.[25] It can be argued that Hussein by no means endorsed the creation of a Jewish state or even an autonomous homeland for the Jews. However, Hussein appears to have been blind to the consequences of the Balfour Declaration.

Hussein also appears to have been ignorant, or pretended

to be so, of the likely post-war settlement, which would see a considerable role for France in the administration of Syria. Mark Sykes, accompanied by Picot, had visited Hussein in April 1917 and given some details of their Agreement. It is a matter of dispute as to how much information was given to Hussein.[26] If he had been in any doubt as to what it contained, the *Manchester Guardian* published it in full on 26 and 28 November 1917 following its leaking by the new Bolshevik government in Russia. This was widely circulated by Jemal, the Turkish governor of Syria. Despite all this evidence, Hussein remained in denial. Reginald Wingate, the High Commissioner in Egypt, wrote that it is 'evident that King Hussein has in no degree abated his original pretensions concerning Syria and apparently still nourishes illusion that through the good offices of His Majesty's Government he may be installed, at any rate nominally, as overlord of [a] greater part of the country'. Wingate tellingly argued against disabusing Hussein of this notion as he might abdicate.[27] Hussein appears to have believed that once the war ended in the Middle East, traditional Anglo-French rivalry would reassert itself and the British would take the side of the Arabs.

Lawrence convinced Feisal 'that his escape was to help the British so much that after the peace they would not be able, for shame, to shoot him down in its fulfillment: while if the Arabs did as I intended, there would no one-sided talk of

> [It is] 'evident that King Hussein has in no degree abated his original pretensions concerning Syria and apparently still nourishes illusion that through the good offices of His Majesty's Government he may be installed, at any rate nominally, as overlord of [a] greater part of the country.'
> REGINALD WINGATE, THE HIGH COMMISSIONER IN EGYPT

shooting. I begged him to trust not in our promises, like his father, but in his own strong performance.'[28] In other words, it was vital for Feisal to make significant military progress to ensure the Arab case was heard at the War's conclusion. As it was, Jemal attempted to break the Anglo-Hashemite alliance by using the Sykes-Picot Agreement as evidence of British perfidy. Feisal received communications from Jemal, and Lawrence agreed that he should respond. Lawrence was aware that Britain was in secret negotiations with conservative elements in the Turkish leadership and did not see why Feisal should not do likewise. Also Lawrence appears to have allowed the correspondence because it was better that it happened with his knowledge than in secret.

Feisal continued to be open to corresponding with Jemal however and in the summer of 1918 Jemal's proposals grew more serious. He was willing to concede independence to Arabia and autonomy to Syria in return for the Arabs changing sides. Lawrence was particularly alarmed by correspondence in June 1918, which outlined Feisal's conditions for a rapprochement with the Turks, which included handing over Amman as well as the Hejaz to Hussein.[29] Lawrence, aware of all this, sent a warning telegram to Hussein, who ordered the ending of the correspondence.

The Collapse of the Ottomans

The Arab Revolt had still not lived up to Hussein's initial claims. Nonetheless, by the spring of 1918, it had killed or captured perhaps 13,000 Ottoman troops. There was also a moral effect on the Arab troops in the Ottoman army facing General Allenby in Palestine. Increasing numbers of them deserted and went home. Also Arab residents in Palestine and in Syria were more welcoming to the British than they might have been if Hussein had remained an Ottoman loyalist. However, Arab military effectiveness remained patchy. In February 1918, for instance, Arab forces failed to capture the strategically-important town of Maan in what is modern-day Jordan. As a result, part of Allenby's Egyptian Expeditionary Force became dangerously exposed and had to abandon Amman – the major town in the Jordan Valley.

After his capture of Jerusalem in December 1917 Allenby had been forced to delay a renewal of his offensive as the Germans launched a major attack on the Western Front in the spring of 1918. It was the end of the summer before he was in a position to renew his attack. With a four to one advantage in frontline troops, Allenby's September offensive was assured of success. The Ottoman army disintegrated within a few days and the British forces with an advance guard of Australian cavalry in the lead began a dash up the Levant. On Allenby's right flank, Feisal's Arab forces swept through the Jordan valley, which had been more or less abandoned by the Turks. There they proved adept at mopping-up the remnants of the Ottoman forces though there were complaints of excessive brutality towards captured Turks. At the same time, the populations of Palestine and Syria now began to rise up and harass the fleeing Turkish forces. A race for Damascus developed between the British spearheads and the Arabs. Lawrence persuaded the Australian commander, General Chauvel, to allow Feisal and his Arab fighters the honour of entering Damascus first. This final *coup de théâtre* ensured that the Arab cause came to the attention of the wider world. It was an immensely political act, Elie Kedourie going as far as to claim that this decision to give Feisal and his followers the honour of entering Damascus as one of the most important influences on Middle Eastern events in the years after 1918.[30]

The Occupation

The British government gave Allenby instructions to treat, so far as military exigencies permitted, the territories captured by the Arabs as Allied 'territory enjoying the status of an independent state (or confederation of States) of friendly Arabs ... and not as enemy provinces in temporary military occupation ...'.[31] When Allenby met with Feisal in Damascus, it was explained that while Feisal was to have the administration of Syria, it was to be a French protectorate. Also the coastal areas from Palestine to the Gulf of Alexandretta were to be under direct French rule. Feisal objected strongly. He did not want to be protected or advised by the French. Lawrence had been told that Sykes-Picot was dead in the water. Now it appeared to be alive and well.[32]

Meanwhile, the French had begun to arrive in the Levant. However, French numbers were puny in comparison to the British – only a few thousand soldiers against nearly a million British and Imperial troops. It was Britannia's writ that ran through the Middle East. Lloyd George was aware of this. He informed the War Cabinet in October 1918 that the Sykes-Picot Agreement was outdated in the new circumstances of an overwhelming British contribution to the conquest of the Middle East.[33] France's influence in the Middle East was based solely on British sufferance. The British conquest of the Levant and the Balfour Declaration had more or less ensured that French aspirations in Palestine were not going to be met. Indeed by the summer of 1918, the French Foreign Office and at least some colonial opinion was of the view that Palestine was lost and the French would have to seek compensation elsewhere. There was also, for annexationists in both France and Britain, the ominous new diplomatic language of President Wilson. Its talk of self-determination and open diplomacy made the implementation of secret deals in the Middle East immensely more complex.

As a result, Feisal was initially in a strong position in Syria. On 30 September 1918, the Allies had created a series of zones in occupied Turkish territory. They were: Occupied Enemy Territory Administration South, made up of Palestine, which the British controlled; Occupied Enemy Territory West, encompassing the coastal littoral of Syria and Lebanon, which French forces were to administer; and Occupied Enemy Territory East, made up of the interior of Syria, which Feisal's Arabs were allowed to control jointly with British forces.[34] In overarching, virtually dictatorial, control of all three sectors was General Allenby. In practice, as he controlled the military forces, the French or Feisal could do little of significance without his agreement. Allenby, though, was extremely concerned about the potential for trouble from the competing ambitions of the Arabs and the French. He confided in a letter to the new Chief of the Imperial General Staff, General Sir Henry Wilson, that he believed that only if the French exercised considerable tact would there be any prospect of placating Arab opinion. He foresaw that politics in the occupied territories, especially in Palestine and Syria would be difficult because of the competing claims of the Jews, Arabs, the European powers and other minorities.[35] Attached to this letter was a memorandum from D G Hogarth of the Arab Bureau. While Hogarth claimed to be happy to leave Syria to the French, he warned that Arab opinion believed that this was incompatible with political independence and that Britain would be accused of having tricked the Arabs into betraying Islam (i.e. the Caliph; the Sultan of Turkey). Britain would also be open to charges of hypocrisy in its repeated declaration of self-determination for small nations.[36]

The first crisis soon arose. Arab forces dashed from Damascus to the capital of the Lebanon, Beirut, and the other coastal towns as Turkish resistance collapsed in early October. An Arab government was proclaimed in these regions. The French, who had been allocated the Lebanon as recently as 30 September 1918, were furious. This, in their mind, was a breach of the wartime agreements. It fuelled suspicions of Feisal and the British. Allenby was forced to accelerate the advance of his troops towards Beirut, as it became increasingly clear that there might be a Franco-Arab clash. Allenby attempted to get Feisal to withdraw. Feisal warned that he might be forced to abdicate if he did not get assurances that the withdrawal would be only temporary and did not imply any abdication of Arab or Hashemite rights in the Lebanon. Feisal was reassured that the divvying-up of the occupation areas was a temporary solution until the Peace Conference had made its decision. This allowed Feisal to give way to the French and let them take over Beirut and the other coastal cities.[37]

Feisal's problems were not simply confined to the Great Powers. The Syria and Lebanon that he occupied had suffered from widespread famine in the previous two years of war. Eyewitnesses spoke of emaciated, hungry children in Beirut 'dying in the gutters'.[38] Influential Damascenes remained suspicious and resentful of the imposition of Feisal upon them by force of arms. The large Christian minorities in both Lebanon and Syria viewed the Hashemites with distaste. An American report on Syria concluded that the country was deeply divided between those who were desirous of immediate annexation of France and those, mainly Muslim, who believed Arabs could rapidly evolve politically and did not require French tutelage. This last group could be driven into the arms of the Turks if the French were not careful.[39] Feisal and his followers attempted to win hearts and minds in the countryside by restarting Ottoman welfare schemes. They also invested some of their British subsidy in buying off Syrian notables. In spite of this, Feisal's authority in Syria was limited.[40]

The British did not ease Feisal's problems by asking him to stay in a military role rather than getting involved in local politics. The British therefore made a Syrian political leader, Ali Riza Pasha, governor of all the occupied territories. Independent-spirited and with no loyalty to Britain, France or Feisal, he began to encroach on French-occupied areas in the Lebanon. Feisal, knowing this was popular with the Syrian population, could not object. However, it significantly impacted on Feisal's ability to get on with the French. The British realised their mistake and removed Riza Pasha at the end of October and transferred his powers to Feisal. However, the Emir remained 'largely a figurehead, which nationalist organisations manipulated for their own purposes'.[41] Indeed, they tended to limit his room for compromise. Feisal was also overburdened with responsibility. He not only had to try to keep control in Syria, he was also to represent the Arabs at the Peace Conference. He would spend a considerable amount of 1919 in Europe. His protégés in Syria, seemingly with little awareness of the political realities, undermined him by seeking political advances far too quickly.

The British and the French continued to appease Arab opinion in the last couple of months of 1918. Perhaps motivated by the continuing fall out from the revelation of the Sykes-Picot Agreements, the disquiet in the Arab world about the Balfour Declaration and the need to impress the Americans that they were committed to the new diplomacy of self-determination, two declarations were issued to the Arabs in 1918. The first was the Declaration to the Seven. The Seven were a small committee of Syrian nationalists whom the British had been in contact with. Issued by Mark Sykes, with official British government approval in mid 1918, it reiterated the recognition of Arab independence in the Arabian Peninsula. Sykes felt he could go no further without French agreement.[42] After discussions between London and Paris, a new Anglo-French Declaration was issued on 9 November 1918. It explicitly committed the British and French to 'the complete and definite emancipation of the peoples so long oppressed by the Turks and the establishment of national governments and administrations deriving their authority from the initiative and free choice of the indigenous populations'.[43] It carefully avoided the use of words like independence. As one commentator has put it, the declaration did not contradict the Sykes-Picot Agreement, 'it only concealed its most crucial details'.[44] Indeed the Declaration was for British ministers not a conversion to the principle of national self-determination but a hard-headed decision to use this new Wilsonian language of diplomacy for traditional balance-of-power ends. In this case it would be used to weaken the French case for territory in the Middle East.[45] The Arab cause, therefore, appeared to be in a very strong position on the eve of Feisal's departure for the Peace Conference. When these promises turned out to be unfulfilled, the Arabs felt an understandable sense of bewilderment and betrayal.

Feisal with his delegates and advisors at the Paris Peace Conference in 1919. Behind him are (left to right) Brigadier General Nuri Said, Captain Pisani of France and Colonel T E Lawrence 'of Arabia'.

II

The Peace Conferences

5
Feisal and the Peace Conference

Feisal leaves for Europe

Feisal realised that he was unlikely to gain the loyalty of the Christians of Syria and Lebanon if he associated the Hashemites and the Arab cause too closely with Islam. Therefore, on 11 November 1918, the day of the Armistice in Europe, he spoke to a large crowd in Aleppo. He denounced the rule of the Ottomans and made clear that the Revolt he led was not motivated by personal or familial aggrandisement nor was he a tool of the Western Powers. Pointing to the Anglo-French declaration he noted that independence would come if the Arabs organised orderly and stable government. The most important emphasis of the speech was his declaration that he was an Arab before anything else. He decried religious sectarianism and declared all religions equal before the law. In the ten days that followed, Feisal toured Syria and Lebanon. He generally received a warm welcome, but in Beirut, with its large Christian population, it was mainly Muslims who welcomed him with enthusiasm, suggesting problems ahead.[1]

On 21 November 1918, Feisal left for Europe on a British

warship. The British government, on the advice of Lawrence, had been convinced that it was in Britain's interests to invite him to the Peace Conference.[2] Feisal would make the Arab case for self-determination and the cause would have a chance of attracting American support. (Lawrence had returned to Europe at the end of October.) King Hussein had agreed that Feisal would act as his plenipotentiary at the Peace Conference. Feisal was accompanied by a small delegation of Arabs, including Nuri al-Said. Lawrence also acted as Feisal's chief adviser. The French were unhappy with Britain's decision to invite Feisal to the Peace Conference. They knew that Feisal coveted all of Syria and were therefore anxious to exclude him. They also knew that Feisal might prove to be an attractive figure to the Americans and their campaign for national self-determination. After their attempt to prevent Feisal coming failed, they tried appeasement. On his arrival in Marseilles, he was decorated with the 'Croix de La Legion d'Honneur' prior to going on a tour of the recent battlefields of the Western Front. He was treated as a distinguished guest but not as a plenipotentiary with the right to speak on behalf of the Arab nation.

An Anglo-French Gentlemen's Agreement

Excluding France from Syria was precisely what many in the British government wanted; none more so than the Lord President of the Council, Lord Curzon. (Curzon ran the Foreign Office for most of 1919 as Arthur Balfour was busy with the Treaties. Curzon became Foreign Secretary in October 1919.) He reflected the widespread view within British government circles that France should not be allowed to straddle British lines of communication to India and the British Empire in the Far East. With German ambitions destroyed, the essential bond between the British and the French was no longer present. Instead Anglo-French relations might revert back to the days of the Fashoda Crisis, when a colonial dispute in the Sudan in 1898 had brought the two powers to the brink of war. Other advocates of using the Arabs to keep the French out of the Middle East included the Arab Bureau in Cairo and Foreign Office officials like Arnold Toynbee.[3] They were given plenty of opportunities to put their case.

T E Lawrence, on his return from the Middle East in November 1918, addressed the British Cabinet's Eastern Committee. He put forward a bold proposal for the administration of the post-war Middle East: that Feisal should administer Syria, and Mesopotamia should be split into two areas under Zaid and Abdullah. The War Office and the Foreign Office were supportive of Lawrence's grand design. However, the India Office, long sick of what they considered the indulgence of the Hashemites by their departmental colleagues, was bitterly opposed.[4] A truncated version of this plan would eventually emerge in 1922 (see Chapter 7). By then Syria would be lost both to the Hashemites and to the wider cause of Arab nationalism.

In the meantime, Lloyd George had become increasingly obsessed with the Middle East. He had begun to view it as a blank canvas on which a new order could be drawn. Greek claims in Asia Minor could be endorsed, as could Jewish demands for a homeland in Palestine. Armenians and Kurds could carve out nation states. Arab states could be established under the tutelage of the British. Egypt would be made a Kingdom under British supervision. Local client states could be cheaply brought under an umbrella of British power. In such a scenario only small forces would be required to maintain British power and influence in the region. What role the French would play in all of this was unclear.

The British would have liked to exclude the French from Middle Eastern arrangements completely. However, this proved impossible. France's involvement in the East had been circumscribed by the need to focus virtually all of its military efforts on the Western Front. Why should French sacrifices against the Germans at the Marne, Verdun and in Champagne be counted as less worthy of reward than the relatively easy victories won by the British in the Middle East? The British, especially Lloyd George, were aware of this claim, though as Britain had borne the brunt of the hardest fighting on the Western Front from mid-1917 this in itself carried little weight. However, the future peace of the world was more likely to be determined by cordial relations between Britain and France than by keeping the Arab cause happy. Lloyd George was to spend the first ten months of 1919 torn between his desire to rearrange the Middle East entirely on British terms and the requirement to keep France as an ally. At times, which goal was the priority was not entirely clear.

On 1 December 1918, Lloyd George and Clemenceau met in London where they made a gentlemen's agreement that was to cement France's rights in the Levant and Syria. In return, Lloyd George secured enhanced gains for Britain. He was determined that Britain's share of the Middle Eastern spoils secured at such great cost in lives and money would be increased. There were more than a million British Empire troops in the Middle East at the end of 1918. Allenby's advance into Syria had been one of the few glorious British victories of the war. Lloyd George made clear to Clemenceau that he wanted control of Palestine and the area around Mosul. Mosul was wanted because of its large deposits of oil and the securing of future oil supplies had become an important aim of British policy, though by no means overarching.[5]

Clemenceau was amenable to these British demands. While acknowledging the problems he might have with his colonial lobby, the French leader replied phlegmatically to Lloyd George's demands. 'You shall have it,' he declared. In truth, Clemenceau did not care much for the French Empire. His main, perhaps sole, interest was in maintaining British support for French demands against the Germans. His submission to Lloyd George's demands was partially in exchange for the Prime Minister's apparently clear backing for Clemenceau's request for a unified French administration for Syria. There were also promises of a share in the spoils of any Middle Eastern oil. There was no formal paper outlining this 'gentlemen's agreement'. Clemenceau had made his concessions. He now wanted to be assured that France's Middle Eastern ambitions would not be wholly thwarted.[6] Lloyd George and the British government, however, were to continue to play the Feisal card, alienating the French and perhaps encouraging their Arab protégé to be more obstinate in his dealings with the French than was wise.

On 4 December, the Eastern Committee met with Lawrence attending again. Curzon fulminated against the Sykes-Picot Agreement, which he now believed had been completely superseded by the new facts on the ground. He saw the Agreement as storing up trouble in the future with Arab opinion. However, the Foreign Secretary Arthur Balfour, aware no doubt of Lloyd George's secret understanding with Clemenceau, declared that Britain could not revisit and amend Sykes-Picot. He took the view that the Agreement could only be scrapped if the Americans pressed for it. As Lawrence's biographer notes, the conclusions of this meeting were that the British Cabinet 'was not prepared to offer Feisal anything more than sympathy.'[7]

OIL IN BRITISH STRATEGY AT THE PEACE NEGOTIATIONS
Prior to the outbreak of war, Winston Churchill, the First Lord of the Admiralty, signalled that the Royal Navy was moving from coal to oil as the main means of ship propulsion and acquired shares in Persian and Mesopotamian oil. During the war Britain was very much dependent on the United States for supplies and the Admiralty was anxious that the British Empire should control at least some of the world's oil reserves. Captain Reginald Hall of Admiralty Intelligence told Gertrude Bell in 1915 'that the ultimate success of the war depended on what we did there', as he pointed at a map of Mesopotamia.[8] However, there is considerable evidence that oil remained a peripheral concern for British negotiators at Paris. It is also true to say that the British government when it considered quitting Iraq in 1921–2 always considered Basra more important than Mosul, which was the oil producing area. Furthermore, within the British government, as influence shifted away from the Admiralty in the post-war era, oil became less of a priority. It was not until the Second World War that oil's overwhelming importance became fully established. After 1945, what had been an important interest became almost an overriding national priority for the British Government.

Undoubtedly, the British government viewed President Wilson's doctrine of national self-determination as a potentially useful tool to keep the French out of Syria. It suited British policy for the time being at least that Feisal get American help rather than British. Their policy was 'to back Feisal and the Arabs as far as we can, up to the point of not alienating the French'.[9] Curzon was also aware that channelling the Hashemites towards Syria rather than Mesopotamia or Palestine had the potential to aid, if not save, British ambitions in the Middle East.[10] At the same time, the French attitude on Syria was hardening. They made clear that they wanted no British discussions with Feisal regarding Syria. Syria, as far as they were concerned, was now a French responsibility and not really a matter for the Peace Conference. When Balfour met Feisal on 12 December, the latter warned him that the

Arabs would go to war against the French over Syria even if the chances of success against a Great Power were negligible. Balfour assured him that his suspicions regarding French plans for Syria had little basis in fact.[11]

Feisal also met Chaim Weizmann while he was in London. They had met before in June 1918, when Weizmann had assured him that the Zionists did not intend to establish a Jewish government in Palestine. He also promised that Jewish money and aid would flow into the region. It is certainly arguable that Weizmann was being disingenuous so that he could secure Arab acquiescence to the Zionist ambition for mass Jewish emigration into Palestine and at the same time prevent the Arabs from opposing the British. Feisal remained acquiescent to the Balfour Declaration, though the Arab and Zionist interpretations of it were considerably different. Feisal was motivated by his anxiety to secure the help of the Jews to lobby the United States on behalf of Arab claims in Syria. Weizmann knew that Arab acquiescence in the Balfour Declaration was the key to its implementation. Feisal was also attracted, as he continued to be for many years, by the lure of large-scale Jewish investment in Palestine. According to Weizmann's account, Feisal did not foresee any problems in future Arab-Jewish relations. However, there remains little evidence that Feisal endorsed or even envisaged any kind of a Jewish state in Palestine.[12] In the last days of December 1918, Feisal and Lawrence began writing the submission that the former would make to the Peace Conference on behalf of the Arabs. It was clear that the Arabs' last hope for independence in Syria was now the United States.

The French government remained determined to exclude Feisal from the Peace Conference, recognising him as an honoured guest but not as a delegate. The reason was that they wanted Feisal to be utterly dependent on them. As a diary fragment from Lawrence in January 1919 confirms, it was touch and go until the last moment as to whether Feisal would be accepted as a delegate. When Balfour proposed a delegation from the Hejaz, Stephen Pichon, the French Foreign Minister, protested. T E Lawrence described how 'Clemenceau accepted one delegate, and Pichon said they could have no more since they were an embryo nationality, not an independent state. Balfour and Lloyd George countered sharply with the statement that they and France had recognised its independence, and the point – two delegates – was carried.' A French Foreign Ministry official, Jean Gout visited Feisal and warned him not to alienate France. Lawrence's account continued: 'He said France was strong, and the sooner Feisal ceased to listen to the mischief-makers in Mesopotamia and Syria who were working against France, the better it would be for him. They recognised no Arab army in Syria, and Allenby lied if he said they did. So Feisal saw that his representation was contested, and spent a very miserable night in consequence. I found him wandering about the hotel at 2 a.m. When we won he took it as a good augury of all the future battles and was very joyful.' [13]

'Much the most dignified presence at the peace conference'

The Paris Peace Conference began in mid-January 1919. A British proposal that the Arab territories captured from Turkey should be subject to what was euphemistically called advice and assistance from the Mandatory Power until they were able to stand on their own two feet was agreed by the Council of Ten. The native populations would receive the right to choose which power would hold the Mandate

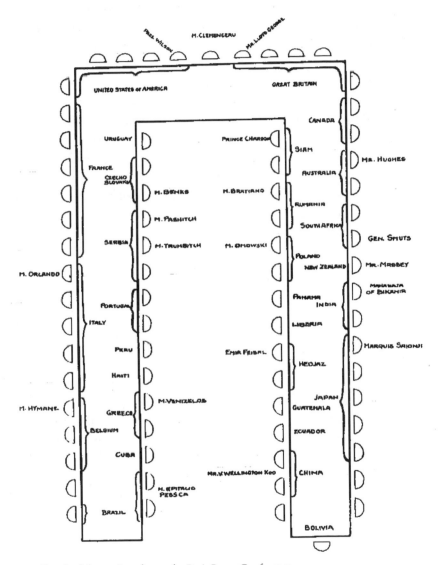

Sketch of the seating plan at the Paris Peace Conference.

over them. The Mandatory system would also be subject to League of Nations supervision. Pichon, the French minister of foreign affairs, proposed in February that France wanted their sphere of influence and area of direct control as proposed under the Sykes-Picot agreement to be amalgamated into a single Mandate. Pichon argued that France's longstanding economic, political and cultural links with the region made her the most suitable Mandatory power. France also expressed a willingness to work with Feisal provided he was willing to accept a large degree of French control over his government. The French had clearly decided that the Mandate system was not significantly different from French colonial practice in Morocco.

Feisal presented his case on 6 February 1919.[14] By then he had already made a favourable impression on many of the assembled delegates. The American Secretary of State Robert Lansing, writing a couple of years later, was lavish in his praise. To another observer, he was 'much the most dignified presence at the peace conference'.[15] Lloyd George was of the view that Feisal's 'intellectual countenance and shining eyes would have made an impression in any assembly'.[16] Stephen Bonsal declared that Emir Feisal, Nuri Pasha and Lawrence 'were certainly the most resplendent figures that had every entered the Quai d'Orsay'. Feisal had come not as a 'supplicant but to demand the rights of his people and the observance of solemn agreements which, as the emergency was over, some were inclined to forget'.[17]

Feisal was well aware that his case had to be strong to attract the sympathy of the United States in particular. He had to prove that Allied plans for the Middle East drawn up during the War were injurious to the right of national self-determination. He also had to prove that the Hashemites were the true leaders of the Arab cause. On this last point he was adamant: *My father has a privileged place among Arabs as the head of their greatest family and as Sherif of Mecca. He is convinced of the ultimate triumph of the ideal of unity, if no attempt is made now to thwart it or to hinder it by dividing the area as spoils of war among the Great Powers.*[18]

Feisal's demands were straightforward – independence for all of the Arabs from the line Alexandretta-Persia southwards. The basis for this demand was that the area constituted a unit suitable for national self-determination. All the inhabitants spoke Arabic, came from the one Semitic stock; there were few nations so homogenous. Furthermore, the Arabs had fought with the Allies, fulfilling their part of the bargain. Now it was time for the Allies to do likewise. Feisal's presentation did contain some exaggerations, however. There were never the 100,000 warriors that he claimed were fielded by the Arabs. While Lloyd George picked some holes in the military contribution of the Arabs, comparing it unfavourably to Britain's commitment of more than a million troops, he remained broadly positive about their case. Pichon's attempt to assert that France had played a major role in the Middle East campaign backfired as Feisal, in the nicest possible way, accurately outlined the insignificant numbers of French troops that had fought in the Middle East.

The Reverend Howard S Bliss, President of the Syrian

'My father has a privileged place among Arabs as the head of their greatest family and as Sherif of Mecca. He is convinced of the ultimate triumph of the ideal of unity, if no attempt is made now to thwart it or to hinder it by dividing the area as spoils of war among the Great Powers.'

FEISAL

FEISAL'S CASE[19]

In his memorandum of 29 January 1919 to the Peace Conference, Feisal asked for the independence of all the Arabic speaking peoples in Asia, from the line Alexandretta-Diarbekir southward.

He based his request on the following points:

(i)   This area was once the home of important civilisations, and its people still have the capacity to play their part in the world.

(ii) All its inhabitants speak one language – Arabic.

(iii) The area has natural frontiers which ensure its unity and its future.

(iv) Its inhabitants are of one stock – the Semitic. Foreigners do not number 1% among them.

(v)   Socially and economically it forms a unit. With each improvement of the means of communication its unity becomes more evident. There are few nations in the world as homogeneous as this.

(vi) The Arabic speaking peoples fought on the side of the Allies in their time of greatest stress, and fulfilled their promises.

(vii) At the end of the war the Allies promised them independence. The Allies had now won the war, and the Arabic speaking peoples thought themselves entitled to independence and worthy of it. It was in accord with the principles laid down by President Wilson and accepted by all the Allies.

(viii) The Arab army fought to win its freedom. It lost heavily: some 20,000 men were killed. Allenby acknowledged its services in his despatches. The army was representative of Arab ideals and was composed of young Syrians, Lebanese, Hejazis, Mesopotamians, Palestinians, and Yemenis.

(ix) The blood of Arab soldiers, the massacres among the civil populations, the economic ruin of the country in the war, deserved recognition.

(x)   In Damascus, Beyrout, Tripoli, Aleppo, Latakia, and the other districts of Syria, the civil [civilian] population declared their independence and hoisted the Arab flag before the Allied troops arrived. The Allied Commander in Chief afterwards insisted that the flag be lowered to install temporary Military Governors. This he explained to the Arabs was provisional, till the Peace Conference settled the future of the country. Had the Arabs known it was in compliance with a secret treaty they would not have permitted it.

(xi) The Syrians who joined the Northern Army were recognised by the Allies as Belligerents. They demanded through this delegation their independence.

Protestant College in Beirut addressed the Council of Ten a week after Feisal. Bliss was Syrian born, but of American ancestry. He urged that a Commission be sent at once to Syria in order to allow Syrians 'to express in a perfectly untrammelled way their political wishes and aspirations, viz: as to what form of Government they desire and as to what power, if any, should be their Mandatory Protecting Power'.[20] Clemenceau was hostile. The French had organised the attendance of a Lebanese Christian delegation, which decried any attempt to impose a primitive Bedouin emir as leader of the advanced races of Syria. Chekri Ganem, the chairman of the pro-French Central Syrian Committee, was brought forward to argue that Syria desperately needed French tutelage.[21] Ganem argued for the separation of Syria from Arabia, as it was a different country and that to 'annex Syria to Arabia would be to do violence to the very soil from which the race and its history have sprung'.[22] The delegation warned of the dangers of allowing the fanatically religious Hejaz to gain control of Syria because its popularity was based on Syrian Muslims seeing it as 'the first foundations of a great Moslem (not Arabian) Empire, with the Hedjaz [sic] dynasty at the head'. Presumably for the benefit of the British, it was pointed out that certain Muslims were seeking 'a further extension of the Empire of Islam, towards Africa and towards India'.[23] Ganem had a point; the various Christian sects concentrated in the Lebanon were wary of Hashemite rule. Indeed the monolithic Arab nation, which Feisal referred to, was much more diverse than he had claimed. Feisal had made considerable attempts to woo Lebanese Christians since he had taken Damascus. Eminent Christians had been offered high-ranking ministerial and diplomatic posts. In spite of Feisal's efforts, it is true to say that this wooing of the Lebanese, and for that matter

Syrian, Christians did not work. No more than a small group of Christians actively supported the Hashemite cause.[24]

However, the French were not simply satisfied with the protection of this minority – they wanted all of Syria. However, Wilson was informed during the course of this presentation, that Mr Ganem's credentials as an objective observer were somewhat undermined by the fact that he had been resident in France for more than three decades. Wilson reacted by pacing the room.[25] He was far more impressed by the Arab case and Feisal in particular. Bonsal heard him say at the end of February 1919: 'Listening to the Emir I think to hear the voice of liberty, a strange, and, I fear, a stray voice coming from Asia.'[26]

> 'Listening to the Emir I think to hear the voice of liberty, a strange, and, I fear, a stray voice coming from Asia.'
>
> **PRESIDENT WILSON**

Arguments continued to rage between the British, French and the Americans. Britain's Colonial Secretary, Lord Milner, handled much of the negotiations with the French. Milner attempted to get the French to negotiate with Feisal. He pointed out the impossibility in the context of a Peace Conference committed to the ideal of self-determination for the French to be imposed on the Arabs of Syria as a Mandatory power. Clemenceau, who was quite detached from the French colonial lobby, was amenable to agreeing some sort of deal with Feisal. Milner explained to Lloyd George on 8 March 1919 that the British position should be to put pressure on both sides to come to some kind of equitable solution. In a letter to Lloyd George, Milner came up with a proposal to resolve the impasse between France and Feisal. France would be given a Mandate over Syria. However, this was to be 'the mildest form of Mandate' and the native population would exercise most of the powers. France would have control over foreign policy and development. Milner, however, was not confident that the French would accept anything short of the 'virtual ownership of Syria'.[27]

Establishment of Commission of Inquiry into Syria

The decisive meeting was held on 20 March 1919. President Wilson, Pichon, Lloyd George, Allenby, and Clemenceau attempted to thrash out the issue of Syria. The French were adamant that Sykes-Picot still stood and that they should receive both Lebanon and Syria. Feisal could be accommodated under this arrangement. Lloyd George took the view that this was based on a misreading of the Agreement. Only Lebanon was to be subject to direct French control and France was bound first to accept that there would be an independent Arab state in the area in the interior of Syria. Lloyd George would not accept direct French control of Syria. Syria, he said, had been promised to the Arabs and British forces had won the war in the Middle East with their help. Allenby warned that the Arabs would revolt if the French attempted to seize Syria, which could destabilise the British position in Palestine, Mesopotamia and Egypt. Wilson now intervened. He declared that the Sykes-Picot Agreement was a dead letter since one party to it, the Russian Empire, no longer existed. He now followed up the suggestion of Bliss and called for an inter-Allied commission to be dispatched to Syria to consult the population. Clemenceau was forced to accept the proposal. The danger of alienating the Americans was too great. He also had to pay lip service to the principle of self-determination. He did insist on the expansion of the commission to look at the wishes of the peoples of Mesopotamia and Iraq, presumably to irritate the British.[28] However,

Clemenceau remained aggrieved towards the British and the following day bitter rows continued over the Syrian question. At one stage, the French leader challenged Lloyd George to a duel.[29] It never took place but Lloyd George, who had two trump cards, the huge British military presence in the Middle East and France's desperate need for a security guarantee from Britain and the United States, was able to win the war of words. Terms of reference for an inter-allied Commission of Inquiry were prepared on 25 March. The terms emphasised the need to discover the sentiments of the Syrians and recommend what territorial divisions would promote peace and development in Syria, Palestine and Mesopotamia.[30] On 29 March, Feisal confided to Wilson's closest adviser Colonel House that the Commission was the best thing that he had heard of in his life. He asked if it were possible for the United States to take over as the Mandatory power in Syria. House was doubtful that America would accept the Mandate.[31]

Feisal's breach with the French

The British were not altogether happy with the Commission of Inquiry, since it might find that the British presence in Mesopotamia and Palestine was unwanted. Indeed, the British High Commissioner in Mesopotamia, Sir Arnold Wilson, was hostile to both Arab nationalism and the Hashemites. He had already carried out a survey, of admittedly dubious authenticity, which had found British direct rule was the preferred option and little support in Mesopotamia for a Hashemite as king. Lloyd George sought to have Mesopotamia excluded from the commission of inquiry on this ground on 27 March.[32] It would appear that pressure was now put on Feisal and the French to come to an agreement that would eliminate the need for an inquiry. The British proposed the Milner formula of 'a mild form of Mandate'. In spite of their concern that Feisal was little more than a British proxy, the French had run out of options at this point. From Feisal's point of view, he now made a disastrous tactical error. Through Lawrence and presumably under considerable British pressure, he told the French that he was willing to accept a French Mandate. He would accept French aid and advisers and cede control over foreign policy, but he wanted Lebanon to be included in a Greater Syria. His motivation for this was that he suspected that the Lebanese Christians would inform the forthcoming Commission that they wished to be protected by France. Feisal feared that he would be left with a land-locked kingdom.

The French now began to see a use for Feisal. Having him on their side would improve Anglo-French relations and most importantly, Feisal had conceded France had a role in all of Syria, not just the coastal region. The French calculated that once they had got their way into Syria, it would be very difficult to remove them. Once French troops were in place, Feisal could either be a puppet or could be expelled at a time of French choosing. France put forward its counter-proposals. While France would accept Greater Syria under Feisal's nominal rule, it was to be federation of tribes and the various religious groups and be subject to the advice of French advisers and soldiers.[33] The French guessed that they would be able to manipulate tribal and sectarian divisions in Syria. They could pursue a policy of divide and conquer.

Clemenceau and Feisal met on 13 April 1919. The former conceded that France would agree to the independence of Syria subject to French troops being admitted to Damascus. Feisal refused. He believed it was a ruse, to allow in a French military presence that would be very hard to dislodge.

Feisal decided to return to Syria the next day. He had come to the conclusion that he would have to rely on the forthcoming inter-Allied Commission to protect the independence of Syria. Feisal had been put under pressure from the British to compromise but he would not trust the French. He rightly believed that they would betray him once they had established a military presence in Damascus.

The French still believed that Feisal was a British puppet. They remained of the view, not entirely without justification that their erstwhile allies were reneging on the December 1918 Lloyd George-Clemenceau agreement under the spurious excuse of supporting self-determination for the Arabs. They noted that the British did not seem overly keen on allowing it in the Middle Eastern areas that they controlled. Moreover, they also considered that Feisal was a dangerous nationalist intent on carving out a large Arabian empire for himself. Clemenceau complained to Colonel House that Lawrence had apparently influenced Feisal's decision to reject the agreement and that a massacre of Christians was being planned by the Arab nationalists in Syria.[34] American delegates had caught sight of a French memorandum on Syria, which revealed that the French expected the Commission to back French goals and the Middle East would be divided on the basis of the Sykes-Picot understanding. An American official commented, 'The Near East is the great loot of the war. The fight on the question of division and mandates must be fought out here in Paris – and the sooner the better.'[35] It would, however, take another year before the Peace Conference would make its final decisions on the settlement of the Middle East.

6

The Collapse of Feisal's Kingdom of Syria

Feisal's concerns

Before he returned to Syria in April 1919, Feisal wrote to Clemenceau. Robert de Caix, a senior French official known for his strong pro-colonial views, rejected Feisal's initial letter, which outlined the demands of the Syrian people and the basis on which he was willing to reach agreement with France.[1] The French, according to British accounts, had become increasingly exercised by what they considered British perfidy against them in Syria. Curzon regretfully reported 'the passionate intensity' with which France meant to stick to 'her Syrian pretensions',[2] Feisal, too, was understandably concerned about the situation. He cabled Allenby in late May about rumours that the international commission was being cancelled and that a large French army was on the way to Syria. He warned that he could not be held responsible for what would happen in such an eventuality but that much blood would be spilt. Allenby, as a result, warned his superiors in London that unless he could reassure Feisal that the Commission would proceed, it was certain that he would raise the Arabs against the French and the British. This would endanger the whole position in Syria and Palestine and Allenby would be unable to handle the situation with the troops at his disposal.[3] These concerns were echoed in a cable from Clayton in Cairo to Curzon, in which he warned that 'violent local disturbances may combine into a general Anti-Christian and Anti-Foreign Movement'.[4] In British-occupied Mesopotamia the view was somewhat different. The Commission was now considered a dangerous initiative and its arrival could 'undermine *defacto* position of European powers in the Middle East, where are [*sic*] military is not so strong that it can afford [to] neglect popular sentiment'.[5]

Feisal placed far too much faith in the power of the Commission of Inquiry to give him control of all of Syria. He also completely overestimated the risks that the British and the Americans were prepared to take to protect him from the French though he sometimes appeared to lurch into despair about his fate and that of Syria. One of his recurring motifs was that he could not understand 'why England should be so afraid of doing anything to offend the country [France], which should logically be prepared to make almost any sacrifice to avoid alienating England'. The result, as one British observer noted was, a lurking suspicion in the Emir's mind 'that the Arabs were being sold'.[6]

Allenby visited Damascus to meet Feisal on 12 May. His arrival was greeted by organised groups of schoolchildren and patriots demonstrating for independence in an attempt to persuade Allenby of the mass popular appeal of Syrian nationalism. Feisal addressed a gathering of notables of Syria. They endorsed a programme of independence, and voted to grant him full powers. He referred to a plan to have a pan-Syrian conference which would declare independence without reference to the Peace Conference. Allenby persuaded him not to do so. According to the British political liaison officer, the 'politicians have only two convictions: firstly they want independence, and secondly that they do not want France. Anti-French feeling is surprisingly strong amongst the people who count, and it is very doubtful whether Feisal would be permitted to bring about a rapprochement even if he wanted to.'[7]

The King-Crane Commission

The Commission of Inquiry nearly did not get off the ground. Increasingly concerned about who garrisoned Syria, Clemenceau demanded that French troops take over from the British in advance of the Commission. Lloyd George refused on the grounds that it would lead to widespread trouble in Syria. However, to stave off a complete collapse in Anglo-French relations and also possibly to forestall the Commission from investigating British rule in Mesopotamia, he agreed that Britain would withdraw from the Commission if France stayed out.[8] Wilson, who had first proposed the idea had, according to one source, 'clean forgotten' about it.[9] After an appeal from Feisal, however, he ordered the American appointees, Henry C King, a college president, and Charles Crane, a businessman, and their staff to proceed with the mission.

The French appear to have viewed the Commission as worthless even before it reported. Picot confided to General Clayton in Cairo that it was a cover 'to keep him [Feisal] in the dark while the partition of Syria is being arranged'.[10] Picot later told Feisal that the Commission had no standing with the Peace Conference and was a private initiative of President Wilson. Feisal refused to accept this interpretation.[11] King and Crane were predisposed to support the French claim for a Mandate informing Wilson that the need for harmony between Britain and France was more important 'than the will of the people of Syria'.[12]

The Commission spent April and May gathering information regarding the region before finally arriving in Jaffa in Palestine in mid-June 1919 and proceeded to travel through Palestine and Syria over the next six weeks. They left for Constantinople on 21 July.[13] The British were informed that they intended to make their stay as short as was possible 'consistent with adequate investigation of the problems before them'.[14] Feisal and his Syrian allies made great efforts to sell the Arab cause to the Commission. Since the establishment of the Arab government in Syria at the end of the War, nationalist elites made up of urban Notables and a middle strata of intellectuals, army officers and professionals were used to administer Feisal's Syria. They designed their greeting of the King-Crane Commission to present 'an image of a sophisticated nation eager and prepared for independence'. However, it is argued that they failed to win the allegiance of the masses.[15] A Syrian Congress was hastily put together. The intention was that this would demonstrate the absolute rejection of French rule by the Arabs of Syria. It was a somewhat imperfect and unrepresentative body. Delegates from French controlled areas were unable to attend and minorities, be they Shias, or Christians, were underrepresented.

Nonetheless King, Crane and their delegation fanned out across the countryside of Syria and Palestine taking soundings from people. They visited more than 30 towns and received thousands of petitions and delegations from villages. There was no ambiguity in the evidence that was presented to the Commission; it was all anti-French. Contrary voices, such as the Maronite Christians from the Lebanon, were excluded mainly by intimidation. The Commission was firmly of the view that there was practically no appetite for a French Mandate in Syria. It also believed that within Syria, 'there is raw material here for a much more promising state than we [the USA] had in the Philippines'.[16] They stated baldly: 'In our judgment proclamation of French Mandate for all Syria would precipitate warfare between Arabs and French, and force Great Britain to dangerous alternative.'[17] Furthermore, 'England would be obliged to choose between Arabs and French with Egypt and India in background'. The only support for a French Mandate came from 'strong parties of Lebanese who demand complete separation of Lebanon with French collaboration'. The Commission was in no doubt that Feisal was the key figure: 'Emir Feisal despite limitation of education has become unique outstanding figure capable of rendering greatest service for world peace. He is heart of Moslem world, with enormous prestige and popularity, confirmed believer in Anglo-Saxon race; real [ly] great lover of Christians [Christianity]. Could do more than any other to reconcile Christians [Christianity] and Islam and longs to do so.'[18]

It is argued that Feisal's manipulation of the Commission to exclude contrary views was a tactical blunder. Furthermore, by placing too much faith in the Commission to the exclusion of accommodation with France, Feisal, according to one hostile critic, 'effectively signed away his imperial dream'.[19] Feisal's faith in the power of the Commission to influence the Peace Conference was encouraged by the British probably to forestall trouble from Feisal and Syrian nationalists.[20]

The Committee reported to the Peace Conference on 28 August 1919. Its recommendations were a serious problem for the policies of the Great Powers. In the most explicit

KEY RECOMMENDATIONS OF THE KING-CRANE COMMISSION[21]
The Commissioners make to the Peace Conference the following recommendations for the treatment of Syria:

1. We recommend, as most important of all, and in strict harmony with our instructions, that whatever foreign administration (whether of one or more powers) is brought into Syria, should come in, not at all as a colonizing Power in the old sense of that term, but as a Mandatory under the League of Nations, with the clear consciousness that 'the well-being and development' of the Syrian people form for it a 'sacred trust'.
2. We recommend, in the second place that the unity of Syria be preserved, in accordance with the earnest petition of the great majority of the people of Syria.
3. We recommend, in the third place, that Syria be placed under on[e] Mandatory Power, as the natural way to secure real and efficient unit.
4. We recommend, in the fourth place, that Emir Feisal be made the head of the new united Syrian State.
5. We recommend, in the fifth place, serious modification of the extreme Zionist Program for Palestine of unlimited immigration of Jews, looking finally to making Palestine distinctly a Jewish State.

Mandatory Power
The Commissioners, recommend, as involved in the logic of the facts that the United States of America be asked to undertake the single Mandate for all Syria. If for any reason the mandate for Syria is not given to America, then the Commissioners recommend, in harmony with the express request of the majority of the Syrian people, that the mandate be given to Great Britain. The tables show that there were 1073 petitions in all Syria for Great Britain as Mandatory, if America did not take the mandate. This is very greatly in excess of any similar expression for the French.

terms imaginable, it made clear that only a small fraction of opinion in Syria favoured a French Mandate. It proposed that America instead take the Mandate, and if it were unwilling that Britain do so. It also urged that the extreme Zionist programme in Palestine be severely truncated.

The deterioration of Feisal's position

The call by the King-Crane Commission for an American Mandate over Syria was simply not in the realm of practical politics. By the end of the summer of 1919, it was becoming increasingly clear that Wilson, thanks to his alienation of his political opponents, would have great difficulty in getting the Treaty of Versailles passed by the US Congress, controlled since the November 1918 election by the opposition Republican Party. Wilson had precious little political capital left. In July 1919 he returned to Washington and in September he began a national campaign for the Treaty of Versailles and the League of Nations. On 26 September 1919, in the midst of an extraordinarily demanding whistle-stop tour promoting the League and the Treaty, he suffered a paralyzing stroke. His political influence essentially ended. Ironically, the day after, the King-Crane Commission report arrived in the White House. It is unlikely that Wilson ever saw it. The Wilsonian internationalist tide was going out. In November 1919 and March 1920, the Senate rejected the Treaty of Versailles. They also declined to take a Mandate over Armenia. Syria, and the idea of an American Mandate over it, was not even discussed by the US Congress. Indeed, General Tasker Bliss, a US delegate to the Peace Conference, had by November 1919 come to the conclusion that American arbitration of Turkish and Middle East problems was 'futile'.[22] The report of the King-Crane Commission was never looked at by the Peace Conference and remained unpublished until 1922.[23]

The strongest British card for defending Feisal – an emphasis on Wilsonian national self-determination – was now essentially a dead letter. Unsurprisingly, the autumn and winter of 1919 saw the British retreat in the face of French demands over Syria. This was in many ways motivated by the demands of the Chief of the Imperial General Staff, Sir Henry Wilson, and the Secretary of State for War, Winston Churchill, for realism by Lloyd George in military affairs.[24] To put it simply, Britain could not afford to maintain its occupation of Syria. The Foreign Secretary Arthur Balfour as early as 19 August and in advance of the King-Crane recommendations, bemoaned the impact of the Syrian question on Anglo-French relations despite Britain's already well-publicised renunciation of any interest in taking a Mandate in Syria.[25] The French press continued to denounce what they considered British attempts to deny France's rights in Syria throughout the summer.

Feisal was also disturbed when Britain made clear to him that it was going to take the Mandate over Palestine and implement the Balfour Declaration. Feisal argued that this was a return to the 'Unjust Agreement of 1916' i.e. the Sykes-Picot Agreement.[26] Arguing that the majority of Arabs had asked for a single Mandate over Mesopotamia and Syria, he warned that if 'there is any possibility of [the] Peace Conference making a decision which is contrary to this desire and which involves a division of country, [he] cannot remain in his present position which would render him liable to the accusation that he consented to the ruin of his country'.[27]

The British, on the basis of hard-headed political calculation, had decided to cut their losses and withdraw their support for Feisal. Since the beginning of the year, one of the more pressing problems for the British government was the expense of the vast military forces that they had deployed both in Europe and the Middle East. Unrest had broken out in Egypt, India, Mesopotamia and Ireland. Britain was facing a very real crisis of empire. Syria was a far lower priority than these regions. Secondly, the British had every intention of enforcing their own Mandate in Mesopotamia. How then, as Balfour noted on 9 September, could Feisal expect a larger measure of independence from the French? He further remarked: 'Neither of us want much less than supreme economic and political control to be exercised no doubt (at least in our case) in friendly and unostentatious co-operation with the Arab – but nevertheless, in the last resort, to be exercised.'[28] Lloyd George consulted with Allenby and the Conservative Party's most influential cabinet minister, Andrew Bonar Law, in a series of meetings in Deauville from 9 to 11 September 1919. A decision was taken to evacuate British forces from the Syrian coast westwards to the Sykes-Picot line. The British subsidy to Feisal would be cut in half and France should take this up. This would all be done by 1 November 1919. Feisal was also instructed to come to France immediately.[29] This was communicated to Clemenceau at a meeting on 15 September. Feisal received the news in person from Lloyd George at 10 Downing Street four days later. Feisal warned that the consequences would be bloodshed.[30]

Feisal was now desperate for some way of avoiding a French occupation. He proposed three alternatives to the British: (1) that Allenby remain in control of the evacuated areas, (2) an international commission to consider temporary arrangement until the Peace Conference had decided, or (3) that the Peace Conference make an immediate decision on the fate of Syria. He also contemplated sending a mission to the United States. In spite of the fact that Arab opinion according to most British reports and the King-Crane Commission had turned very strongly against any significant Jewish settlement in Palestine, Feisal met again with Weizmann, who proposed that in exchange for his backing of the Zionist project, the Zionist movement could provide advisers and money to the Arab government. Feisal was inclined to accept the agreement provided the Zionists joined with the Arabs against the French, but Weizmann was reluctant to break with the French arguing that they could be squeezed out of the coastal parts of Syria later.[31]

It was inevitable that Feisal, under considerable British pressure, would once more turn to the French. Lloyd George asked Clemenceau to avoid treating 'Feisal and the Arab problem with a high hand. If this were indeed the policy of the French Government, the British Government are afraid that it would inevitably lead to serious and long continued disturbances throughout the Arab territories which might easily spread to the whole Mohammedan world.'[32] Clemenceau took note of Lloyd George's views and began to moderate French aims. The objective remained to protect French imperial designs but now crucially an attempt would be made to satisfy Feisal and the British. Notably, Clemenceau prevented the French commander in Syria, General Gouraud, from occupying the Bekka Valley.[33] However, when Feisal and Clemenceau met in October and November there was no meeting of minds between them on the issue of sovereignty over Syria. Clemenceau was determined that French troops would occupy Syria and French administrators would have virtual *carte blanche* to run the country as they pleased. Feisal rejected this proposal.

However, Clemenceau and the French decided to make significant concessions, and new proposals were presented to Feisal on 16 December. Now in return for the French having the sole monopoly over provision of military and civilian advisers, which would be responsible to the Syrian government and Feisal's acknowledgment of France as the Mandatory Power, Syria would have an independent parliament with the right to levy taxes and make laws and Feisal would be recognised as head of the new Syrian state. Additionally, France agreed not to station troops in the Arab part of Syria without the consent of the government. Feisal agreed these terms on 6 January 1920. However, Feisal had to secure popular support within Syria for the French Mandate before the Lebanon would be handed over.[34] The agreement was kept secret. A French official who communicated the terms to the British claimed the French 'were rather nervous as to whether Feisal would be able to maintain his position on his return to Syria and for this reason the agreement was to be kept secret at present and Feisal was to return with an ostensibly clear hand'.[35]

Undoubtedly, Feisal was extremely unhappy with the agreement. He almost certainly realized that it would be difficult to sell to the radical nationalists, whose influence in Syria was steadily increasing. Conversely, Gouraud saw the new agreement as a defeat for France. He foresaw that the agreement would be interpreted by the Arabs as providing for their complete independence without any French influence.

The situation in Syria

Feisal's political influence in Syria was never all that strong. There were nationalist undercurrents there over which Feisal had little control. His second trip to Europe at the end of 1919 reduced even this limited influence. Gertrude Bell, a member of the Arab Bureau, identified some of these problems when she visited Syria in October 1919. In her view things were falling apart as the Arab government had refused help or advice from the French while at the same time the British could not help for fear of damaging relations with the French. Therefore, she noted 'they go their own way and their way is not good'.[36] The main centres of power were three nationalist groups: the mainly Palestinian Arab Club (*al-Nadi al-'Arabi*), the Syrian-led *al-Fatat*, which controlled the Arab Independence Party (*Hizb al-Istiqlal al'Arabi*), and *al-Ahd*, which was made up of Iraqi members of the Ottoman army who had defected to the Arab Revolt. These organisations sometimes worked together for the Arab cause. Often though, they displayed more loyalty to their regional or tribal interest. In such a factional atmosphere there was also a tendency for these groupings to attempt to outbid each other with displays of nationalist fervour, which limited Feisal's room for compromise with the French.

The men left in control by Feisal and who dominated his brother Zeid were mainly from *al-Ahd*, whose key figure was Yasin Pasha al-Hashimi.[37] In Bell's view they were 'violent Nationalists and are out for an independent Syria and Mesopotamia without any foreign control'.[38] Her summary of the state of opinion in Damascus was that Feisal had lost ground.[39] In a despatch written at the end of her visit she noted the sense of growing despair about the future in the Syrian capital. 'Damascenes are exceedingly anxious at the prospect which lies before them. At the end of the year the subsidy to the Sherif will cease and the financial position of the Arab Government will be extremely precarious but even if it can contrive to keep itself in existence and succeed in preventing open disorder it is anticipated that the

Gertrude Margaret Lowthian Bell (1868–1926), traveller, archaeologist, Arabist and diplomat. A member of a rich Durham family, Bell travelled widely across the Middle East prior to the First World War. In 1915, she joined the Arab Bureau. A late convert to the idea that the Arabs were capable of self-government, she became a major influence on British policymaking in the Middle East especially the eventual settlement of Britain's relations with Iraq. She remained an adviser to the Iraqi government until just prior to her death, though her influence on it and British policy had begun to decline.

French in the coast provinces will foster disturbances, either by the continuance of propaganda within the Arab State, or by provocative acts towards Moslems in the area under their administration, and that on the first breach of the peace their troops will cross the frontier on the plea of restoring order.'[40]

When Feisal returned with his deal, he found that it commanded little popular support among nationalists. Another problem was the resignation of Clemenceau as French Premier soon after the agreement was put into practice. The French elections at the end of 1919 had produced a conservative majority that had little interest in appeasing Arab opinion. The new French Premier, Alexandre Millerand, was of the view that France had already conceded too much to Feisal. There was also the problem that Syrian nationalists and independent bandits were stepping up attacks on French forces, which angered the French government. Gouraud had no confidence in Feisal and believed that he was in the hands of the most radical nationalist elements in Syria. The British were positive about the agreement but saw little prospect that Feisal would be able to implement it. As Lloyd George noted at an Allied conference in February 1920, Feisal was not in 'a consenting frame of mind'.[41]

Events bore out this gloomy assessment. Feisal was caught between the demands of the French and the Syrian nationalists. He desperately sought more concessions from Millerand. Specifically he sought increased independence in foreign policy and a reduction in the size of the Lebanese state, but Millerand rebuffed the approach. On the contrary, the French premier wanted the accords of 6 January to be amended to grant France even greater influence and control in Syria. His preference was for the division of Syria along ethnic and tribal lines, leaving it with a powerless centre. Feisal was now left with an ever-decreasing set of options. He either had to go completely over to the French and sanction the use of their troops to crush Syrian nationalists or he had to abandon all dealings with them and go over to active opposition. British reports noted the enormous pressure he was under from the extremist party. His father Hussein, perhaps out of envy of Feisal's successes, warned he would repudiate any agreement with France that did not safeguard Arab independence.

Yasin Pasha al-Hashimi, who exercised considerable influence over Feisal, had strongly opposed any pact with the French and led street demonstrations in January 1920 against the Feisal-Clemenceau agreement. Feisal's appeals for moderation fell on deaf ears. The nationalist cause meanwhile had given every nationalist but also every bandit license to carry out attacks, especially in the coastal area.[42] Christians and other minorities in Damascus lived in fear of being massacred. Feisal was obliged to reconvene the Syrian National Congress that had been formed for the visit of the King-Crane Commission on 6 March 1920. It remained absolutely uncompromising in its nationalist views. It declared Feisal's accord with the French null and void and declared independence with Feisal as Head of State. Palestine was proclaimed part of the new kingdom. Some time later Abdullah, Feisal's older brother was proclaimed King of Mesopotamia. Feisal, as he had warned the British, had to go along with the nationalist tide or be overthrown.[43]

Appeals were made to other governments for recognition. The French saw the declarations by the Syrian nationalists as conclusive evidence that Feisal had endorsed the views of the extremists. In the Lebanon, Christian groupings, no doubt with the encouragement of the French, proclaimed their independence from this new Syrian state. The British also suggested that Feisal's support in Damascus among Christians and the Druze was quite weak.[44] Millerand was determined that the declarations of the Syrian Congress would not stand. The British were now very much in step with the French; Lord Curzon, Foreign Secretary since the autumn of 1919, told them that the declarations were 'an unwarranted and intolerable exercise of authority' by the Syrian Congress. However, Curzon also took the opportunity to berate the French for imperiling the British and French positions in the Middle East by 'forcing themselves into areas where the French were not welcomed by the inhabitants'.[45] The British were especially concerned by the Syrian Congress's claims in Palestine and Mesopotamia. Lloyd George, though, seemed to be favourable to the idea and Allenby argued that Britain and France should recognise Feisal as sovereign over a confederation of Syria, Palestine and Mesopotamia while tying them administratively to Britain and France. Curzon, though, felt the plan was unclear and that consultations in Mesopotamia in 1919 had suggested that there was little appetite for a Sherifian ruler.[46]

Feisal appears not to have been concerned enough by the warnings issued by the British and French. Instead, the French were brusquely informed that they must recognise Syrian independence and withdraw their forces from the Lebanon before he would return to Europe. Superficially, Feisal's position remained strong. The French appeared to have insufficient troops on the ground to drive the nationalists out. The British remained reticent about an assault on Feisal and the French also had the problem of Cilicia to the north of Syria, which Mustafa Kemal and his nationalist Turkish forces (the Kemalists) were beginning to menace. In early 1920, a French force was routed. Until these problems were resolved, there was no prospect of moving against Feisal.

However, in reality, Feisal's position was much weaker than it seemed. According to his own testimony, he was more or less forced into acceding to the independence declaration or face losing his crown. Indeed, he hoped the declaration would sate popular opinion in Syria and provide a breathing space by which he could negotiate a deal with the British and French. There were many in Syrian nationalist circles who would like to have made common cause with the Kemalists.[47] Furthermore, the military and economic position was desperate.[48] There were food riots in Hama just four days after the declaration of independence. Food shortages, rising prices and currency problems became increasingly acute. Politically, Feisal's position was weak. His ability to compromise with the French, which he almost certainly favoured, was constrained by extreme nationalists who brooked no compromise.

San Remo

The Middle East had largely disappeared from the agenda of the Peace Conference after May 1919. Other settlements were more pressing. In June 1919, the Treaty of Versailles had been signed with Germany. Subsequently treaties were signed with Austria (St Germain, 10 September 1919), and Bulgaria (Neuilly, 27 November 1919). The Paris Peace Conference ended on 21 January 1920 with the first meeting of the new international body aimed at preserving peace – the League of Nations. (In 1920, further treaties with Hungary [Trianon, 4 June 1920] and the Ottoman Empire [Sèvres, 10 August 1920] would be finalised and signed.)

A meeting of the Peace Conference in late April 1920 at San Remo in Italy was earmarked to deal with the Middle Eastern Mandates and prepare the groundwork for the Turkish peace treaty. The French also viewed the meeting as a means of clearing away the obstacles to intervention against Feisal and indeed the problem with Britain was largely dealt with at San Remo. Curzon tried to fight a rearguard action on Feisal's behalf. His suggestion that if Feisal came to the Peace Conference, agreed to accept a proper Mandate and came to a final agreement with the French and British regarding the status Syria and Palestine, the Allies should recognise him as King of Syria, was unacceptable to Millerand. He was not willing to concede that France would have a weak mandate in Syria, while Britain would have much greater freedom of action in Palestine and Mesopotamia. When Millerand threatened to revisit the status of Palestine, suggesting that the idea of an international regime should be brought back on the agenda, Curzon agreed that Britain would recognise French Mandates in Syria and the Lebanon in return for their recognition of the British Mandates in Mesopotamia and Palestine. Britain was resigned to France dealing with Syria as it pleased. Feisal himself had refused to go to San Remo, sending his chief of staff Nuri al-Said instead. Nuri, however, had been unable to influence the deliberations.

Nuri al-Said (1888–1958), army officer and Iraqi politician. He agreed to join the Arab Revolt in 1916, and became Feisal's chief of staff. He spent a considerable period of time in Europe at the peace conferences at Paris and San Remo. After Feisal's deposition in July 1920, he played an important role in helping him achieve the crown of Iraq. After helping establish an Iraqi army, Nuri first became Prime Minister in 1930. A strong advocate of close and harmonious relations with Britain, by the mid-1940s he had become the dominant figure in Iraqi politics. However, his closeness to Britain made him a hate figure for radical Arab nationalists, and he was brutally murdered in the 1958 Iraqi revolution.

The end of Feisal's kingdom

After San Remo, Millerand moved to prepare the ground for an assault on Syria. General Gouraud was ordered to encourage the development of local autonomy in the country. He had advocated such a strategy earlier in the year. Gouraud also sent Robert de Caix to parley with Mustafa Kemal. A cease-fire was secured at the end of May, giving Gouraud a free hand to concentrate his forces against Feisal and the Syrians. The French plan was simple. Feisal was to be presented with an ultimatum to end all attacks on the French by Arab groups. Should this not be immediately complied with, French forces would occupy Damascus and Allepo, disarm the Syrian forces and depose him. It would appear Millerand relished the opportunity to finish with Feisal once and for all. Substantial reinforcements were sent to the Lebanon to prepare for a military solution. Gouraud was equally enthusiastic to end the 'phoney war'. French agents also sought allies among the Syrians. There were a number of groups in Syria that were anxious to see the back of Feisal's regime, the Druze and Christian populations being the most notable collaborators with the French.

On 18 May, Curzon appeared to abandon any pretense of support for Syria. While still asking that the French show moderation in their treatment of Feisal, for fear that they would drive him into the hands of the Turkish nationalists, it was recognised that France was the best judge of the 'military measures' to meet the local situation and that it had the right to use such measures.[49] The following day, the French government resolved to crush Feisal and the Syrian nationalists by force. Appropriate orders were issued to General Gouraud on 22 May. He was promised considerable reinforcements that would arrive in time for a military strike in July.[50] All other French aims in the Middle East became subordinated to gaining control of Syria. Gouraud was instructed to renounce or put on hold French rights in Cilicia to secure his flank from attack by the Turks, and a truce with Kemal was concluded on 1 June. By the end of June, the French had assembled sufficient forces in the Levant for a strike at Damascus.

Feisal was by now aware of French forces massing on the frontier of Syria and that France was seeking allies among Syrian notables and tribal leaders. He again sought to compromise and began to rein in the activities of the guerrillas. Similarly, the Damascus press and political parties were brought under tighter supervision. This repression was put in place to prevent any incident that would provide an excuse for the French to march on Damascus.[51] He also sent Nuri al-Said to parley with Gouraud.

Gouraud, with his forces in place and anxious to force the issue, wanted Feisal isolated in Damascus. He feared that Feisal might prevent an attack by either making a deal with Paris or securing another British intervention. Either occurrence might cheat him of the final reckoning that he now desired. Gouraud sent Nuri back to Damascus on 11 July with new and unpalatable demands including French occupation of the Rayaq-Aleppo railroad, acceptance of the Mandate and the end of military conscription. Feisal rejected the demands. In response to Arab reinforcement of the border with the French zone, Gouraud moved forces into Rayaq. On 14 July, Gouraud sent a written ultimatum to Feisal demanding he accept the 11 July terms and outlining how Feisal and the Syrian nationalists had failed to comply with previous agreements. Feisal had five days to respond or face invasion and French military occupation. Feisal made last desperate appeals to Britain to intervene. The British urged caution on the French but as Lord Hardinge, the Permanent Under-secretary at the Foreign Office, noted, it was impossible for Britain to intervene as a result of the San Remo agreements. In his view, if the French treatment of Feisal led to trouble in the future it would be better that the responsibility should lie solely with them and that the British were not implicated.[52]

War fever now spread through the unoccupied part of Syria. Despite some desertions, the bulk of the military officers around Feisal remained steadfast and determined to fight. However, the army was an army in name only. It was desperately short of heavy weapons, and while rifles were plentiful, ammunition was in very short supply. Feisal's attempts at negotiations with Gouraud yielded a few concessions but the French commander still made demands for the punishment of extremists, which included high-ranking officials in the army. Feisal agreed to virtually the entire French ultimatum. He began to make preparations for a military crackdown against extremists who would almost certainly oppose his capitulation. Feisal suppressed the Syrian Congress when it opposed his acceptance of the French terms, leading to an outbreak of street fighting in Damascus, which troops loyal to Feisal crushed with great force.

Gouraud, however, appears to have been playing Feisal along. On 20 July he declared that Feisal had not complied sufficiently with French demands despite desperate efforts to do so. French forces moved against Syria just after midnight of that day. Feisal, after a final and fruitless attempt to negotiate, decided to stand and fight. Arab forces attempted to block the French advance at Maysalun near Damascus. The French had more troops as well as tanks, aircraft and superior artillery. The result was the inevitable rout of the Arab forces. Feisal returned to Damascus. Gouraud and the French now had no use for him and he was told to leave. On 1 August, Feisal and his entourage left for Europe via Haifa. Syria was now completely in French hands. Gouraud immediately implemented a divide-and-rule strategy by creating autonomous areas in Syria that would emphasise tribal, religious and ethnic divisions to facilitate French rule. The dream of an Arab kingdom in Syria was now gone forever. Feisal appeared to be just another nationalist that the Western Powers no longer had any use for – destined to be forgotten.

King Abdullah of Transjordan (left) and his host and former bitter enemy, King Ibn Saud of Saudia Arabia, are seen together at Riyadh, 29 July 1948.

III

The Legacy

7
Reversals of Fortune 1920–5

After the debacle in Syria, it would not have been any great surprise if the world had never heard of Feisal again. However, within a year, the British government had come to the conclusion that he was the only possible candidate to be ruler of strife-torn Iraq and his election as Iraqi King was arranged. This astonishing change of fortune was driven by the necessity of the British to create ruling structures in Iraq that would allow Britain to retain its influence there but at a much lower cost. More or less at the same time, Abdullah was allowed to establish himself as Emir of Transjordan. This occurred because of the same financial constraints on the British and the need to have some plan for the desert territory east of the Jordan that the British appear to have envisaged as forming part of Feisal's Kingdom in Syria. By the mid-1920s, Feisal and Abdullah were firmly established as rulers in the British Mandates of Iraq and Transjordan. Hussein, however, who maintained lingering hopes that he would be ruler of a wider Arab entity in the Middle East was to lose the kingdom he had established in the Hejaz and was to end his life in bitter exile in Cyprus.

The Hashemite Kingdom of Arabia

In October 1916, the *Ulema*, the leading Muslim scholars, in Mecca had declared Hussein King of the Arab Nation and religious chief until Muslims were of one opinion concerning the fate of the Islamic Caliphate. Hussein's claim for leadership of all Arabs was not widely accepted by many Arabs, or, indeed by his main sponsor, the British government. The British were disturbed by the hubris of his claims and would only recognise Hussein as King of the Hejaz.

During the Arab Revolt, power began to drain away from Hussein to Feisal, of whose successes he became increasingly jealous. In August 1918 a furious row had broken out between Hussein and Feisal, who threatened to resign as military commander, and only Lawrence's mediation prevented it from developing into a full-blown crisis. During the Syrian crisis of early 1920, Hussein had undermined Feisal's attempts to compromise with the French, seemingly oblivious to the realities of the situation.

Within the Hejaz itself, Hussein's position was not that strong. His other rivals in the Arabian peninsula, especially 'Abd al-'Aziz Ibn Saud, had also been strengthened by the war. Ibn Saud had risen to prominence in 1902 when a force he led captured the city of Riyadh in Central Arabia from Ibn Rashid. This success allowed him to make himself Emir of Nejd. He continued to expand his territory and by 1914 he was the most significant power in Central Arabia and was essentially independent of the Ottomans. Ibn Saud was an adherent to the particularly austere Wahhabi sect of Sunni Islam, which was founded in the 18th century by Muhammad ibn 'Abd al-Wahhab (1703–92), who formed an alliance with the Sauds. By 1806, most of the Arabian Peninsula including Mecca and Medina had been conquered. Eventually forces from Egypt crushed the Sauds and the Wahhabis. The family's fortunes did not recover until the early 20th century when Ibn Saud launched his wave of conquest.

The religious zeal of the Wahhabis provided considerable societal cohesion in the Nejd. Any sort of cohesion, other than a universal willingness to accept Hussein's subsidies and bribes, was singularly absent in the Hejaz. Ibn Saud also forged a new instrument of state building and military power with his creation of the quasi-military religious brotherhood called the *Ikhwan*. The *Ikhwan*, mostly former nomads, established settlements in the Nejd in which they founded *madrassas* (religious schools) and cultivated land. However, they could quickly be mobilised to terrorise Ibn Saud's internal and external enemies.[1] Hussein and Abdullah were both well aware of the growing threat of Saud. While Ibn Saud had carefully husbanded the British subsidy he had received during the War, Hussein had lavished his on both the Arab Revolt and on bribing tribes to stay out of Ibn Saud's orbit. Abdullah's lack of participation in the Arab Revolt is partly explained by his fear that Ibn Saud would take advantage of Hussein's commitment to it to further his power.[2]

The Khurma dispute[3]
In 1914, the Emir Khalid of the Utayba tribe in the Khurma region, to the east of Jeddah, had converted to Wahhabism. He remained under Hussein's political influence and participated in the Arab Revolt. However, in 1917 Khalid fell out with Abdullah and began to assert his independence by refusing to fight anymore or pay taxes. He also sought aid from Ibn Saud though Saud demurred from providing it. Hussein also became increasingly concerned about British encouragement of Ibn Saud to attack the Ottoman supporter, Ibn Rashid,

which he saw as threat to his pre-eminent position among the Arabs. At the root of it all was Hussein's desire to have Ibn Saud excluded from the war effort against the Ottomans. He wanted the British to be overwhelmingly dependent on him, but they, while leaning towards Hussein, also wanted to keep Ibn Saud as an ally and continued to cultivate him.

Hussein was determined to enforce his will in Khurma by military force. His first attempt to do so was rebuffed by Khalid and local forces in July 1918. *Ikhwan* warriors began to move into Khurma to aid their co-religionists and Ibn Saud became increasingly committed to supporting its independence from Hussein. Leadership in the Arabian Peninsula in the early 20th century grew out of the barrel of a gun. If he could not suppress recalcitrant tribes such as the Utayba in Khurma, Hussein's claims to primacy would inevitably fail. In May 1919 following the long-delayed surrender of the Ottoman garrison at Medina, Abdullah was sent with a Hejazi army to try to suppress Khurma once more. Abdullah had not gone north to Syria with Feisal because he viewed Hashemite ambitions in the Arabian Peninsula as more important than those in Syria and Mesopotamia. He had concluded that the end of hostilities with the Ottomans was merely a pause before a future conflict with Ibn Saud for supremacy in the Arabian Peninsula. However, on 25 May 1919, Abdullah's better armed and equipped army of 3,000 men was surprised by a night attack on their camp at Turaba spearheaded by *Ikwhan* warriors. The army, including its heavy equipment, was virtually destroyed; Abdullah only just escaped with his life.[4]

Hussein's power in the Arabian Peninsula was now severely diminished. Only British pressure on Ibn Saud prevented him pressing home his advantage. The British went so far as to prepare contingency plans to intervene. Ibn Saud, as usual, demonstrated commendable restraint and did not push his military advantage to its obvious conclusion. He remained anxious to remain on good terms with the British. As a British government memorandum written a couple of years later noted 'there is no doubt had he so desired, Ibn Saud could have taken Mecca and overrun the Hejaz'.[5] Feisal, in control of Syria at this time, fearful that France would take the opportunity to attack should he rush to his father's aid, was unable to help. Hussein became ever more anxious after Turaba that Syria should be linked to the Hejaz, as the viability of the Hejaz as an independent kingdom was always doubtful. The limitations of Hashemite power and Hussein's lack of leadership skills had been all too evident in the Khurma affair.

The British considered that Hussein had been the cause of most of his own troubles by failing to parley with Ibn Saud. Lord Curzon now saw Britain's erstwhile ally as 'a pampered and querulous nuisance'.[6] His sons, particularly Abdullah and Feisal, were estranged from him; Feisal, because of his success, and Abdullah as a result of the disaster at Turaba. His eldest son Ali, who remained at his father's side in Mecca, believed that the temperamental behaviour of his father was isolating him and was increasingly dangerous to the Arab cause.[7]

The consequences of the defeat at Turaba were exacerbated by a growing financial crisis for Hussein. Since 1916, Hussein had become utterly dependent on the British financial subsidy. The subsidy proved to be an additional 'Achilles heel' for him, however, for such was the lavishness with which he bribed tribes, he created the expectation that such largesse would continue for ever. The bribes also only bought temporary loyalty. When the British government began to reduce the subsidy, Hussein found his ability to maintain tribal influence in the Hejaz and neighbouring parts of Arabia severely diminished.[8] Indeed, the financial crisis cost him support in the Hejaz as he was forced to tax the merchants and traders of Jeddah and Mecca in order to fund himself. The people of the Hejaz were used to receiving money from the Ottomans, not having to pay it out. By mid-1920 Hussein was receiving only £30,000 in gold a month from the British as opposed to over £200,000 at the height of the war.

In August 1920, the British requested that Hussein sign up to the Treaty of Versailles and the arrangements agreed at San Remo the previous April in return for further funding. Hussein adamantly refused. The British spent the next four years attempting to formalise their relationship with Hussein by means of a bilateral treaty. Lawrence met him in July and August 1921, tasked with persuading him to accept British terms. Hussein was his usual contradictory self. Lawrence commented: 'The old man is conceited to a degree, greedy and stupid, but very friendly, and protests devotion to our interests.'[9] The fact was that Hussein was increasingly convinced that the British had let him down over the post-war settlement and in his conflict with Ibn Saud. Despite Lawrence's entreaties, Hussein refused to sign any treaty until the British had recognised his kingship of Palestine and Iraq and priority over all rulers in Arabia. Lawrence eventually left.

The refusal to agree a treaty prevented Hussein receiving any further British support. It was a foolish decision and a fatal error.[10] While Ibn Saud had created a socially and military cohesive state in central Arabia, Hussein had relied for legitimacy on his diplomatic skill and ability to win international support. The combination of military failure, incompetent governance and the rejection of overtures from Britain, his main sponsor, left his kingdom extremely vulnerable to further attack from his great enemy, Ibn Saud.

Abdullah and Transjordan

Of Hussein's sons, Abdullah is often credited with having the most political intelligence. However, as a military commander, he demonstrated little talent either during the Arab Revolt or the campaign in Khurma. The defeat at Turaba ended what ambitions that he may have entertained of carving out a kingdom for himself in the Yemen or the centre of the Arabian Peninsula at the expense of Ibn Saud. Abdullah now looked northwards. Like his father, he felt considerable antipathy towards Feisal for his successes in Syria. In early 1920, his gaze turned towards Baghdad where he hoped, in vain as it turned out, that the British might appoint him king. At this stage, however, the British authorities in Baghdad were implacably hostile to the Hashemites (see below).[11]

In August 1920, Hashemite ambitions suffered a further setback when the French offensive in Syria forced Feisal into exile. Abdullah decided to move north with some 2,000 followers to join other Arab nationalists who were rallying with the aim of reversing the French coup. Abdullah established himself in November 1920 in the small town of Maan. However, he proved himself a master of inaction and it was clear that a move against the French was not really on his agenda at all.[12] It had no chance of success. The area where Abdullah and his forces proposed to operate from was in the British zone and lay roughly within the boundaries of the modern state of Jordan, an area which the British referred to as Transjordan. The British had assigned the area to Feisal under the occupation arrangements in late 1918. The French, having rid themselves of Feisal, had no desire to see his supporters operating against them in this area and they proposed to move in to occupy it. The British warned them off and reasserted their rights to the region. Herbert Samuel, the British High Commissioner in Palestine, favoured incorporating the area into the Palestine Mandate. The British, however, had very little military power on the ground to deal with the Arab nationalists who had moved into Transjordan. An unsatisfactory situation now arose with the British unsure of what to do with Abdullah.[13] A decision was taken to leave Abdullah temporarily in charge. The French continued to complain about the ongoing infiltration of Arab fighters into Syria from Abdullah's territory, with his apparent acquiescence. However, the fate of the barren region of Transjordan was of minor concern to the British government in comparison to the much higher stakes being played for in Mesopotamia.

The Mesopotamian problem

The territories that form modern-day Iraq (generally referred to as Mesopotamia until August 1921) had been incorporated into the Ottoman Empire in the 16th and 17th centuries. Three administrative divisions, centred on the major towns of Mosul, Baghdad and Basra, were established. However, Ottoman rule was weak, power being exercised via a military elite of *mamluk* pashas who enjoyed considerable freedom of action.

The three provinces had a wide variety of peoples and religious groupings within them. Overall, and unusually for an Arab region, there was a slight majority of adherents to the Shia branch of Islam. Arabic-speaking Sunni Muslims were in a considerable minority – around a quarter of the population. However, considerable regional differences existed in the spread of the population. Around Mosul and in the north, Kurdish speakers made up a large segment of the population; the city of Baghdad was a polyglot city with a large number of Sunnis and Shias, as well as the Middle East's largest urban population of Jews; while around Basra and in the south, the population was overwhelmingly Shia, though the ruling elite tended to be Sunni. The most sacred centres of Shia worship, the towns of Karbala and Najaf, were concentrated in southern Mesopotamia.

From the 1830s, Ottoman rule over the three provinces was strengthened as part of the *Tanzimat* reforms, with the *mamluks* replaced by Ottoman governors. As elsewhere, the increasing centralisation of power of the Ottomans, which threatened to undermine the tribal system, led to outbreaks of revolt. The Ottomans were forced to rely on divide and conquer tactics to secure their rule. The three provinces were also affected by the Young Turk revolution of 1908, which gave rise to a flowering of clubs, parties and newspapers, many with nationalist or devolutionist agendas. However, as in other Arab-speaking regions, local hopes of increased decentralisation were dashed by the emergence of the centralising CUP as the dominant political force in Istanbul.

In November 1914 an Anglo-Indian Mesopotamian Expeditionary Force (MEF) had seized Basra. The aim of the occupation was to protect British interests at the head of the Persian Gulf. However, the mission of the MEF was expanded. All of Basra province was occupied in early 1915 and this encouraged the MEF to move forward towards Baghdad. However, 50 miles short of Baghdad, a large British force was stopped and surrounded at Kut, where it surrendered in early 1916. The British now advanced much more slowly. It was March 1917 before Baghdad was captured and the northern areas of what is modern-day Iraq were not taken until near the end of the War. During the War, as in most Arab areas, the bulk of the population in the three provinces stayed either loyal to the Ottomans or indifferent to the struggle. The most significant nationalist input was the recruitment by the British of numbers of captured Ottoman Mesopotamian troops to the Arab Revolt. While these were few in number, they exerted influence beyond their numbers in the upper echelons of the Arab Revolt, especially after Feisal became its leader.

As the British advanced into Mesopotamia, what to do with the captured territories became an increasing concern. From the start, British opinion was united that Mesopotamia should be under British control. However, the extent of this control was a matter of some dispute. In Delhi, the British Indian government saw the lightly populated areas around Basra as a possible colony for Indians and a potential breadbasket. They were adamantly opposed to any independence for the captured territories and were determined to exclude the Hashemites from Mesopotamia. The High Commissioner of the conquered territories was Percy Cox, until May 1918 when he was sent on a lengthy mission to Persia. He had established relative calm in the occupied territories. His view, and that of his Oriental Secretary, Gertrude Bell, was that permanent direct British rule was the best means of maintaining peace and order. But Cox's replacement, Sir Arnold Wilson, strongly supported the anti-independence and anti-Hashemite views of the British Indian government. Wilson was also opposed to the Anglo-French declaration of November 1918, as he believed it would not only fail in its objective of keeping the French out of Syria but would also cause the British difficulty in Mesopotamia.

The Eastern Committee of the British Cabinet, chaired by

Lord Curzon, was more sympathetic to the Hashemites. T E Lawrence, whose views echoed those of the Arab Bureau in Cairo, made a presentation arguing for a Hashemite ruler in Mesopotamia in November 1918. Conflicting opinions on the Eastern Committee, in any case, prevented any serious examination of these proposals, while Wilson, in Baghdad, went out of his way to frustrate any attempt to bring a Hashemite into Mesopotamia. As noted earlier, he carried out a survey of popular opinion in Mesopotamia, which concluded that there was no appetite for a Hashemite ruler and the preferred option was for continued British rule. Baghdad was the exception to this view. It is not clear to what extent Wilson manipulated his survey but in any case Curzon enthusiastically accepted the result. Feisal, however, who had Mesopotamian officers with him in Baghdad, wrote to Curzon in June 1919 warning of the danger of ignoring their concerns about the lack of any British attempt to engage with nationalists.[14] His action and other propaganda efforts in Mesopotamia by Feisal and his supporters' aroused considerable concern in both Baghdad and London.[15]

By the end of 1919 there was growing opposition to foreign rule in Mesopotamia as it became clear that the British had every intention of ignoring nationalist aspirations. Gertrude Bell had changed her mind about the fitness of the Arabs for some form of autonomy. She was now of the firm view that there would be a violent explosion unless these aspirations were met but her views were in a small minority within the Mesopotamian Political Service (the title of the British administration in Iraq), to which she had been assigned at the conclusion of the First World War.[16] One group that was especially resistant to British blandishments was the Shia clergy. The powerful Sadr family was described by Bell as 'bitterly pan-Islamic, anti-British *et tout le bataclan*'.[17] (The Sadr family would be influential Shia opponents of the US-UK occupation after the March 2003 invasion.) By mid-April 1920, Bell felt that a major nationalist demonstration against British rule was imminent. Her sympathies now lay with the nationalists.[18]

Tension was significantly heightened in the spring and summer of 1920 by the decisions taken at San Remo, which confirmed the Mandate system and the partition of the Arab world, the French attack on Feisal and the publication of the terms of the Turkish peace treaty, which seemed to suggest that the Caliphate would be ended and that the hour of destruction of the Islamic faith was at hand. In a series of apparently uncoordinated outbursts beginning in early June 1920, Sunni nationalists in Baghdad, Shia religious elders in the holy cities and tribal leaders along the Euphrates rose in revolt. However, while the revolt involved most of the major groupings in Mesopotamia, saw major disturbances in more than a third of the countryside and inflicted hundreds of casualties on the British, it failed to seize any of the major cities. The dispersed nature of the revolt allowed the British to pick off the centres of resistance one by one. Finally, there was no figurehead or leader to rally and coordinate the uprising.[19] By the end of August, the revolt was, in the main, defeated.

The British Cabinet lost confidence in High Commissioner Wilson and his strategy as a result of the enormous human and financial cost of the revolt. A memo in July argued for the sacking of Wilson and the establishment of a Royal Commission to ascertain the best form of administration for Mesopotamia.[20] Leading the criticism was T E Lawrence, who made a number of forceful attacks in the British press on British policy and on High Commissioner Wilson.[21] The view that

Wilson was out of his depth was widespread and a decision was taken to bring Percy Cox back. However, due to his other commitments this could not be done until October 1920.

Churchill's Strategy

In 1920, the key players in the formation of British policy were the Prime Minister Lloyd George, the Chancellor of the Exchequer Austen Chamberlain, the Colonial Secretary Lord Milner, the Foreign Secretary Lord Curzon, the Secretary of State for India Edwin Montagu and the Secretary of State for War Winston Churchill. Churchill was the strongest opponent within the British Cabinet to the strategy being pursued in Mesopotamia. Since the end of the war, he had been under great pressure to find economies and savings in British expenditure and the huge British military establishment in Mesopotamia, which had stood at 255,000 troops and support staff in August 1919, was his favoured target for cuts.[22] Indeed he was sceptical about the decision to partition the Ottoman Empire as it was 'abetting a crime against freedom in deserting and, it will be alleged, betraying those Arabs who fought so bravely with us in the war and immensely expensive'. Britain would be better off investing in developing its existing Empire instead of wasting money on enlargements, he believed.[23] The cost of the military establishment in Mesopotamia continued to exercise him during the first half of 1920 as the cost of suppressing the rebellion, which amounted to nearly £40 million, became a domestic issue when the press baron Lord Rothermere's Anti-Waste League used it as an example of government profligacy.

The pressure to cut military expenditure in Mesopotamia now required a reversal of policy. Direct rule from London or Delhi was no longer a feasible strategy and there was an urgent need to install a reliable Arab regime that would limit British expenditure in Iraq.[24] At the end of December 1920, the Cabinet discussed a proposal from Percy Cox, who had resumed his old job as High Commissioner of Mesopotamia, that Feisal be proposed as King of Mesopotamia to sate nationalist sentiment and allow a significant reduction in the British garrison.[25] Despite the disaster in Syria, Feisal still had considerable respect and numerous supporters within the upper echelons of the British government including the Prime Minister, Curzon and Hardinge, the Permanent Under-secretary at the Foreign Office. Indeed Curzon would have activated the 'Feisal as King of Mesopotamia' option sooner had it not been for French objections.[26]

The alternative to this strategy was far more unpalatable. This was to withdraw British forces to Basra and leave the rest of Mesopotamia to Mustafa Kemal's Turkish nationalists or even anarchy.[27] Churchill's alternative strategy for reducing expenditure was to use air power. He succeeded in persuading Lloyd George that prescriptive (or perhaps more accurately, terror) bombing of recalcitrant Mesopotamian villages would allow significant savings in the number of troops required to hold the region. Combined with Cox's political strategy to provide an Arab government that would command the loyalty of the population and reduce the requirement for troops, massive expenditure savings could be made.

Churchill's coherent cost-saving strategy in Mesopotamia made him an obvious choice to deal with the crisis in the British Mandates in the Middle East. Therefore, when Lord Milner indicated his desire to be relieved of the Colonial Office, Lloyd George decided to replace him with Churchill in January 1921. Churchill moved swiftly. He rapidly concluded that Feisal was the best man for the job of ruling Iraq. He also fast-tracked moves to streamline decision-making in the Middle East. Churchill was convinced that a single sub-department of the Colonial Office was the best solution, 'otherwise muddle, failure and discredit are certain'.[28] Since 1917, the British had wrestled with how to run their policy in the Middle East, which according to Mark Sykes had some 18 different organisations and groups providing input.[29] Now there was to be a single voice under the control of Churchill. While Curzon was irritated and suspected Churchill of a Middle Eastern power-grab, there must also have been a certain sense of relief that the troublesome area was now someone else's problem.

The Middle East Department of the Colonial Office came into being on 1 March 1921. It was given responsibility for the British Mandates, the Arabian Peninsula and Persia. The first Under-Secretary was John Shuckburgh, an India Office hand with significant experience of the Middle East. T E Lawrence agreed to be Churchill's Middle Eastern adviser.[30] Both Lawrence and Hubert Young, the head of the political and administrative branch of the new department were pro-Hashemite 'partisans'.[31] However, their appointment reflected the need to have officials on board who would be able to woo the Hashemites and implement the new British strategy.

The key British link to Feisal remained, of course, Lawrence. He had been initially sceptical about helping the British government after what he felt was the betrayal of the Arabs at the Peace Conference. However, he met privately with Feisal to ascertain his views. The Emir was willing to work with the British though concerned that both Abdullah and his father might object.[32] His strategy having some prospect of success, Churchill now decided to hold a conference in early March 1920 of all of the British Middle Eastern experts in Cairo that would focus on what to do with the Mesopotamian Mandate.

The objectives were: to formally endorse a new Arab ruler; to formulate a timetable for the reduction in size of the British garrison to a more economical peacetime establishment; to calculate future financial aid for the Mandate; and to decide which parts of Mesopotamia were worth retaining.[33] On his way to Cairo, Churchill met the French who reiterated their objections to Feisal being made King of Mesopotamia. However, the British no longer felt much beholden to the French on this issue.

The Cairo Conference[34]

The venue for the conference was the Semiramis Hotel. Beginning on 12 March 1921, for 12 days over the course of more than 40 secret sessions, some 40 British Middle Eastern experts and policy-makers – including all of the high commissioners, the senior regional military commanders, the political residents, and governors of territories such as Somaliland – worked through an agenda that would shape the Middle East to the present day. It was rapidly agreed that in Mesopotamia, which was to be renamed Iraq, Feisal offered the best and most economical chance of success. Percy Cox and Gertrude Bell were both supportive but they proposed that Feisal should be seen to be the choice of the Iraqi people rather than be imposed. A formula was agreed that Feisal would announce his availability to serve as King of Iraq and the British government would state that it would not stand in his way.[35]

The conference also considered the question of Palestine. Herbert Samuel, the High Commissioner, was still in favour of a Mandate encompassing all of Palestine and Transjordan, arguing that this was what the Balfour Declaration had said and that the creation of a separate Mandate might lead to complications with the League of Nations. The question became more urgent when news reached the conference that Abdullah had advanced to Amman. It was now clear to Churchill that an agreement would have to be reached with him.

When Churchill and Lawrence went north to Jerusalem at the conclusion of the conference, a meeting was arranged with the Emir. Churchill told Abdullah that Transjordan would not be part of Palestine. Abdullah was offered a leadership role in Transjordan and a subsidy. In return he was to stop attacking the French. He would also receive British advisors and a promise of eventual progress towards independence.[36] Abdullah was also persuaded to waive his claims to Iraq. There was also an intimation that if he behaved well, the French might approach him and give him a role in Damascus, though Antonius suggests that this was a trick to keep him quiet.[37]

> 'What had begun as an exercise in pragmatism had been expanded at Cairo into a principle to be applied wherever possible, beginning with Mesopotamia and then spreading to Arabia and Transjordan.'
> **AARON KLIEMAN**

The most notable impact of the conference was that the 'Sherifian Solution' became the new British strategy for managing the Middle East. As Aaron Klieman notes; 'What had begun as an exercise in pragmatism had been expanded at Cairo into a principle to be applied wherever possible, beginning with Mesopotamia and then spreading to Arabia and Transjordan.'[38]

Events now moved swiftly as the British sought to implement their plan. Lawrence told Feisal to make his way to the Middle East. On 15 April, they had a long conversation in which Feisal agreed that he would not attack the French in Syria, and would seek to compromise with Ibn Saud provided he did not attack his father in the Hejaz. He also fully acknowledged that he would need British advice and support in Iraq as the population there was not yet ready for self-government.[39] The British agreed with him, Churchill envisaging that Iraq would be run 'much like an Indian state'.[40] Percy Cox and Gertrude Bell prepared for Feisal's arrival. She organised everything from the Emir's travel arrangements to the design of a temporary flag for the new state. The main potential domestic opponent of Feisal was Sayid Talib. After he was reported to have expressed displeasure at the turn of events, he was arrested and sent into permanent exile in Ceylon.

Feisal arrived in Baghdad on 23 June 1921. The Iraqi Council of Ministers, under Cox's direction, ratified Feisal as candidate and a plebiscite was arranged for August. Ninety-six per cent pronounced themselves in favour of Feisal, but there was no way that Feisal actually had that level of support. There were large numbers of pro-Turkish groupings who wanted close links with Mustafa Kemal, Shias who wanted a theocracy and Kurds who desired independence. However, Feisal was probably the least worse option. As Phebe Marr notes, 'there is little doubt that no other candidate had his stature or could have received anywhere near the acclamation he did'.[41] Feisal was crowned as Iraq's first monarch on 23 August 1921.

The 'Sherifian Solution' comes under strain

The League of Nations ratified the Mandates for Iraq, Palestine and Jordan in July 1922. This was followed by an Anglo-Iraqi treaty that was ratified in October. The negotiation of this treaty was to strain relations between the British and

Feisal to breaking point. Feisal had learned much from his experiences since the end of the War, particularly his vulnerability to the machinations of the Great Powers. Despite this, he remained determined that the British and the native Iraqi Notables would not leave him a powerless constitutional figurehead and looked for opportunities to extend his power.[42] His main internal support came from the entourage of Sherifian officers who had served with him during the Arab Revolt and in Syria, and who he installed in positions of power and influence in Baghdad. The most notable, Ali Jaudat and Nuri al-Said, were to be the dominant figures in Iraqi politics for the next 37 years.

It was not long before Feisal faced his first crisis. The British had decided at Cairo that the Mandatory relationship between Britain and Iraq would be outlined in a treaty. In theory it would not be a British *diktat*, though in practice that was exactly what it was. When Feisal started to make objections to certain aspects of the proposed treaty, particularly Britain's control of Iraqi international relations and the formal abrogation of the Mandate, a crisis in Anglo-Iraqi relations arose that was to last for much of the first year of Feisal's reign. Feisal's delaying tactics caused Churchill to complain that it was only six months since Britain was paying his hotel bill and now he had to read lengthy telegrams reporting Feisal's questions on his and Iraq's status.[43] The stand-off finally came to a head in the summer of 1922. By August 1922, Cox was of the view that Feisal had taken up with the extremist party and was no longer the right man for the throne. Cox proposed that he should hold elections and place the treaty before the assembly. If it was rejected, Britain should quit Iraq with the exception of Basra. Churchill held much the same view, arguing to Lloyd George that any government that got the Iraqi burden off its back would gain popularity. Further-more, he saw no point in Britain paying £8 million 'for the privilege of living on an ungrateful volcano out of which we are in no circumstances to get anything worth having'. Lloyd George rejected a 'policy of scuttle'.[44] Feisal might well have been toppled had he not been stricken by appendicitis. This allowed Cox to assume full control of the government, arrest the main extremist nationalist agitators against the treaty and force the Iraqi Council of Ministers to ratify it in October. Relations between Cox and Feisal were soon restored to an even keel. It was an extremely fortuitous bout of appendicitis for Feisal.

Abdullah was having problems with the British as well. He failed to impose any kind of law and order in Transjordan and was harbouring anti-French forces. General Congreve, the British commander in Transjordan, wrote Churchill in August 1921 calling for Abdullah, who in his view was a fraud and a knave, to be kicked out. There was still talk that the French were considering Abdullah for a role in Syria, though this was unlikely. Lawrence, on a mission to King Hussein, was sent to organise Abdullah's departure. However, Abdul-lah, who until now had been positively unenthusiastic about his position in Transjordan, requested to stay.[45] It was not until May 1923 that Abdullah was fully secure in power, when the British recognised the Emirate of Transjordan as a national state being prepared for eventual independence by them.[46]

The signing of this agreement caused King Hussein to fly into one of his by-now characteristic rages. Already estranged from Feisal by his acceptance of the crown of Iraq and a truce with Ibn Saud, he now furiously denounced Abdullah. He believed Abdullah's deal with the British acknowledged Jewish claims in Palestine and more importantly, in his now extraordinarily egocentric view of the world, denied his own claims to rule Transjordan. Abdullah, unlike Feisal, was still strongly under the influence of his father and when he met him in January 1924, was so bullied and dominated by him that the British feared that the Emir might give up his claims in Transjordan in favour of Hussein. By now that was the last thing they wanted to see.

Hussein made one final blunder. In spite of his financial and military weakness, he took the opportunity provided by the abolition of the Caliphate by the Turkish National Assembly in March 1924 to declare himself Caliph. The action attracted support in Syria and in Transjordan where Abdullah canvassed on behalf of his father. However, in Iraq and Saudi Arabia, there was rejection and outrage. Ibn Saud's *Ikwhan* warriors demanded that they be allowed to move against the Hejaz once and for all. In August 1924, Ibn Saud launched an offensive that rapidly took the towns of Taif and Mecca. Hussein abdicated in favour of his eldest son, Ali, though he continued to interfere from Akaba. Only Medina and Jeddah remained in Hashemite hands. Ibn Saud's forces blockaded Jeddah for more than a year. The foolishness of Hussein's decision to abandon his alliance with Britain was demonstrated when British military intervention routed an *Ikhwan* raid aimed at toppling Abdullah in 1924.[47] Ali might well have saved his regime too. Instead, on 5 December 1925, Medina surrendered. This set off a mutiny amongst Ali's troops in Jeddah. Most of the Jeddah notables were by now willing to submit to Ibn Saud. Ali gave in to the inevitable and abdicated on 19 December 1925. The Kingdom of the Hejaz now ceased to exist. Ibn Saud and the *Ikhwan* remained a threat to both Transjordan and Iraq. It was not until 1928 that Ibn Saud accepted the borders with Abdullah and suspicion and mistrust would continue down the years between the two leading dynasties of the Middle East.

8

The Peace Treaties and the Fate of the Arab Lands

Five major political entities were established in the Arab world by the decisions of the Peace Conference and its long drawn-out aftermath. These were the British Mandates of Iraq, Transjordan and Palestine, and the French Mandates of Lebanon and Syria. Three other fully independent states also emerged: the Hashemite Kingdom of Arabia (the Hejaz), the Yemen and Ibn Saud's Sultanate of Nejd and its dependencies in Central Arabia. In North Africa, Arab populated Egypt became a quasi-independent Kingdom in 1922, but Britain continued to intervene in its internal politics and maintained the Suez Canal base and other military facilities equivalent in size to Wales until 1951. Around the southern and western coasts of the Arabian Peninsula, a series of small emirates continued to enjoy British protection. The most notable were Kuwait, the Trucial States, Oman and the various sheikdoms in the hinterland of the British controlled port at Aden. In Arabia, Ibn Saud, as noted earlier, ended Hashemite rule in the Hejaz in December 1925. He was proclaimed King of the Hejaz in early 1926. He also

Turkey and the Near East 1923

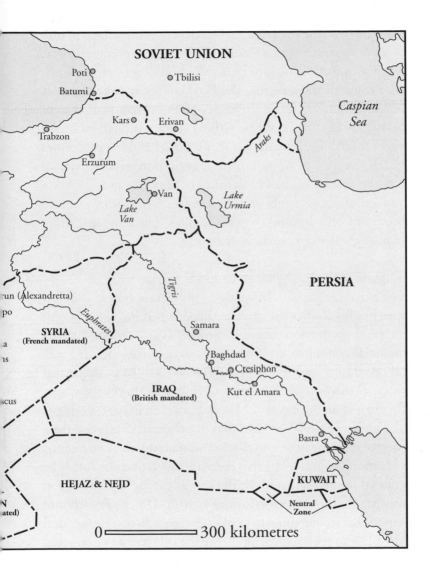

continued to rule the Nejd and its dependencies. This fiction of two separate entities continued until September 1932, when a unitary Kingdom of Saudi Arabia was proclaimed. As a result of these events, the Hashemites and the al-Sauds remained bitter rivals until the common threat of President Nasser of Egypt's brand of radical Arab nationalism in the 1950s forced a reconciliation. Both Feisal and his successors in Iraq as well as Abdullah in Transjordan believed that it was the destiny of the Hashemites to regain control of Syria and bring about Arab unity. However, Arab unity was to prove not only beyond the Hashemites, but also their more radical challengers, such as Nasser.

Iraq under the Hashemites to 1945[1]

The 1920s saw rapid political developments in Iraq after Feisal was finally confirmed on the throne. Britain was content to speed up the devolution of power, as it would reduce its financial commitment. The Anglo-Iraqi treaty of 1922 was followed by a supplementary agreement in 1924. The major external threat to the integrity of Iraq was Turkey's claim to the old Ottoman *vilayet* of Mosul. However, in 1925, a League of Nations commission declared in favour of continued Iraqi control over the area and Turkey accepted this. The League of Nation's commission also recommended that the Kurds be granted limited self-rule. In the same year, an oil concession was granted to a consortium of British, Dutch, French and American oil companies to exploit the large discoveries around Mosul. Iraq received royalties for the oil that was extracted though its demand for an actual share of the company was rebuffed.[2] This provided revenue to the government from the 1930s reaching some £84.6 million a year by 1958.[3]

Relations between the Iraqi leadership and Britain

remained strained over the ending of the Mandate and over issues such as the introduction of conscription, especially between 1926 and 1929.[4] The election of a Labour government in Britain in 1929 saw an increased appetite on the part of Britain to advance Iraqi independence. In 1930, a new Anglo-Iraqi treaty was signed. In return for rights to military bases and guarantees for economic and oil interests, the British government agreed to recommend the termination of the Mandate and to support Iraqi entry into the League of Nations. This was achieved in 1932 and Iraq became the first of the Mandates to achieve independence. British advisers were now employees of the Iraqi government and no longer able to veto government policy. The Prime Minister at the time of formal independence was Nuri al-Said. He proved to be the strong man of Hashemite Iraq. Right from the start he silenced opposition from those opposed to any continued British influence.[5]

Feisal remained acutely aware of the underlying weakness of a regime that was dominated by Sunni Arabs in a land where they made up less than a quarter of the population. For this and for wider Arab nationalist reasons, Feisal continued to pursue wider pan-Arab ambitions. In short he still wished to control Syria. If a union of the Fertile Crescent could be established with him at its head, the Shias and Kurds would be minorities in this wider entity. Furthermore, many of his key advisers and staff were Syrians who had come to Iraq. Perhaps the most important was the Yemenese-Syrian Sati al-Husri, who became Minister for Education. Part of the role of the embryonic school system of Iraq, which al-Husri developed, was to be 'a tool for nationalist indoctrination'.[6] However, Feisal, well aware of previous setbacks, was careful not to push pan-Arabism too far. For instance, he was reticent about supporting the 1925 Druze-led revolt in Syria. Nonetheless, Feisal complained about provisions of the 1930 Anglo-Iraqi treaty because they seemed to preclude the unification of the Arab-speaking states of the Middle East. Feisal, the British High Commissioner Francis Humphrys noted in 1930, 'still hopes and works for the close federation under the rule of his House of all the Arab territories in Asia, and it seems that his intention is to endeavour to bring about first the union of Syria and Iraq'.[7] The Sunni elite at the pinnacle of Iraqi politics envisaged Iraq as the Piedmont or Prussia of the Arab world which would drive forward the cause of pan-Arabism. One of the biggest political issues was conscription, which the King and the Sunni elite also viewed as a means of nation-building in their ethnically-divided country. For this reason, the Shias and Kurdish populations were strongly opposed, as were the British who saw it as both financially and ethnically destablising.[8]

There were other claimants for the mantle of leader of the Arab world. Feisal's brother, Abdullah, who had consolidated his rule in Transjordan by the end of the 1920s, envisaged a role for himself in Syria. Indeed, as we have seen, he had stopped in Transjordan on his way to confront the French in Syria in 1920 and then hung on there in anticipation of being called to take the throne of Syria. He saw himself as the leader of any Hashemite restoration in Syria. His prospects were improved by the death of Feisal I of Iraq after a short illness in 1933. By then the Hashemite monarchy in Iraq was running into increased difficulties including sectarian problems with Shias, Kurds and the tiny Assyrian community. The last named were crushed with great brutality in a pogrom in 1933. The army was regularly called upon to put down tribal revolts in the Shia areas in the south of Iraq with the same heavy handedness, especially after the introduction of conscription in 1933. This gave the army leadership increasing political influence. In 1936, after Yasin al-Hashimi, the Prime Minister, began to demonstrate increasing authoritarian tendencies, General Bakr Sidqi, encouraged by Hashimi's enemies, staged a coup. King Ghazi, Feisal's young son and successor, did not especially object to the coup once the monarchy was not threatened. In any case, Ghazi tended to be in sympathy with the nationalist officer corps and lacked his father's political realism. Most importantly, the coup was a huge blow to constitutional rule in Iraq and signalled the beginning of violent faction-fighting among the Sunni elite.[9] Sidqi was assassinated in August 1937 and the older establishment figures such as Nuri al-Said and Rashid Ali returned to positions of power. However, from 1937 until 1941, despite the holding of elections, the arbiter of power in Iraq was a nationalist army clique known as 'the Golden Square'. Civilian governments fell if they incurred the displeasure of this group. This 'Golden Square' held pro-Nazi and anti-British views, which were greatly heightened by the anti-British/anti-Zionist revolt in the Palestine Mandate between 1936 and 1939.

In 1939 Ghazi died in a car crash. His successor was his young son, Faisal II. Abdullah, son of Ali ibn Hussein the last king of the Hejaz, became regent. He was by instinct pro-British. Consequently, tensions between the royal family and the nationalist officers in the army grew from the outbreak of the Second World War. These were exacerbated by British demands for full Iraqi compliance with their obligations under the 1930 treaty including the breaking of diplomatic relations with the Axis Powers. In the spring of 1941 Abdullah was forced to flee after months of political infighting culminated in the seizing of power by the nationalist Rashid Ali, who enjoyed the confidence of the 'Golden Square'. The British, convinced of a German-Italian plot to drive them from the Middle East, decided to secure their positions in the region. In a matter of a few weeks in late April and May 1941, British forces landed at Basra and toppled the Rashid Ali regime. In June, they moved against Syria and expelled the Vichy Governor (see below). A second British occupation of Iraq followed and a pro-British ruling group around the regent was re-installed. Those who had opposed the British, such as Rashid Ali, found themselves exiled and excluded from power. His supporters who stayed behind were executed or imprisoned.[10] Nuri al-Said backed the British and became the dominant political figure in post-1941 Iraq. He viewed the British connection as an important support for the Hashemite monarchy in Iraq and its wider ambitions in the Middle East.

Abdullah's ambitions for a pan-Arab state

A strong supporter of the British reconquest of the Middle East during the Second World War was Emir Abdullah of Transjordan who provided military support via his British-trained Arab Legion. Abdullah, by default, was now *de facto* leader of the Hashemite family. However, he ruled the weakest of the Arab states and the one most dependent on British support. Transjordan remained desperately poor and underdeveloped. With a tiny population, lacking oil or other natural resources, Abdullah, even more so than his relatives in Iraq, considered it necessary to further his ambitions by merging Transjordan in a wider Arab entity. For one thing, it would allow him to throw off the shackles of the British. He was anxious that he should have a leading role in the post-war settlement of the Middle East when it was assumed that the Mandate system would come to an end. It was believed by Abdullah, and by virtually all pan-Arabists, that this would presage the union of all of the Arab countries in the Fertile Crescent (Iraq, Syria, Transjordan and Palestine).

Abdullah was anxious for talks on Arab unity to take place before Transjordan, Syria, Palestine and Lebanon became independent. Fearful that he would be too weak to achieve union on his own, he decided that his best chance of success was to co-operate with the British and hope that they would use their enhanced influence in Syria after 1941 to get him the throne there. However, Abdullah was mistrusted by much nationalist opinion in the Arab world as a British stooge.[11] Abdullah's big plan was to create a Greater Syria, essentially a Syrian-Jordanian federation. However, Syrian nationalist leaders such as Faris al-Khouri were reluctant to commit while vestiges of French influence remained. Shukri al-Quwwatli, the President of Syria, rejected Abdullah's overtures decisively in 1946 and the creation of the Arab League in March 1945 gave Egypt an increasingly important role in Arab unity discussions. The British themselves had little interest in backing Abdullah in Syria. While they had come to the view that Abdullah was one of Britain's most useful Middle Eastern allies, they were sceptical about his wider regional ambitions. Abdullah's reward came in 1946 by having Transjordan granted formal independence and renamed the Hashemite Kingdom of Jordan. Emir Abdullah was now King Abdullah.

Abdullah now turned his attention to Palestine. He had long had an ambiguous relationship with both the British Mandatory authorities in Palestine and the representatives of the Jewish population, which had grown enormously in the 1920s and 1930s. It would appear likely that his preference was for some sort of Jewish autonomy within a wider

Hashemite federation. It became clear that this was not going to happen as Jewish violence against the Mandate authorities and the Palestinians increased at the end of the Second World War. Abdullah appears to have decided, with the encouragement of the British government, to secure at least part of the Palestinian Mandate in the aftermath of a British departure. Furthermore, in November 1947 an unofficial *modus vivendi* was agreed between Adbullah and the Jewish leader David Ben-Gurion. According to this, Abdullah was allowed to seize the West Bank of the Palestinian Mandate in return for not bringing the full weight of his forces against the fledgling Jewish state. This plan was strongly supported by the British who wished to strengthen Abdullah and frustrate the Grand Mufti of Jerusalem, Hajj Amin al-Husayni, whom the British viewed with distaste for his role in the Palestinian rebellion between 1936 and 1939 and for his links to the Nazis during the Second World War.[12] The exact origins of the partition of Palestine between Israel and Jordan remain the subject of heated historical debate. However, the facts on the ground were clear. The new state of Israel seized nearly 80 per cent of the old Palestine Mandate, while Abdullah was able to secure for himself the West Bank including East Jerusalem, which he formally annexed in 1950. Jordan also received a large proportion of the 750,000 Palestinian refugees created by the 1947–9 fighting in Palestine.

Abdullah viewed the creation of Israel more phlegmatically than the other Arab states, and Jordanian and Israeli negotiators maintained discreet contacts after the war. These negotiations included proposals for a final partition of Palestine that would include a Jordanian corridor to the Mediterranean and a non-aggression pact. However, there was strong opposition within his government and in the wider

Arab world. Israel was also unwilling to make the necessary territorial concessions to make an agreement work. These talks came to an abrupt conclusion with the assassination of Abdullah by an extremist Muslim outside the al-Aska Mosque in Jerusalem on 20 July 1951.[13]

Abdullah's immediate successor, his son Talal, was forced to abdicate in August 1952 due to mental illness. Hussein, Talal's son, was only 17 when he succeeded him. For the first 20 years of his reign, recurring crises threatened the monarchy, but Hussein proved to be one of the most extraordinary survivors that the Middle East has ever seen, despite his instinctive and occasionally impetuous policymaking. With no oil and a recalcitrant Palestinian population that disliked the Hashemites, he managed to survive a series of desperate crises in 1957 and 1958, partly orchestrated by President Nasser of Egypt, as well as defeat in the 1967 Middle Eastern War.

Hussein's gravest error was to join Nasser in the 1967 War against Israel, which cost Jordan the West Bank and East Jerusalem and caused another huge influx of Palestinian refugees into his kingdom. In the aftermath Palestinian *fedayeen* guerrillas created a state within a state and openly defied Hussein. Their raids on Israel, which drew massive military retaliation and the hijacking of Western airliners in September 1970, compelled the King to act. In ten days of bitter fighting, the Palestinian guerrilla groups were eliminated or forced out. After this, Hussein's regime was relatively stable. When the Palestinians and Israelis signed the Oslo Accords in September 1993, Hussein rapidly moved to conclude an agreement with the Israelis that finally terminated the 46-year state of war. He died in 1999. Perhaps his greatest achievement was that he was able to pass on a relatively stable kingdom to his son, Abdullah. Few would once have imagined this possible.[14]

Nuri al-Said, Nasser and the end of Hashemite power in Iraq

In contrast to Abdullah's willingness to seek peace with Israel, Iraq, despite its pro-Western orientation, was militantly opposed to any compromise with the new state. The year 1948 was a very unsettled year for the country. Severe riots erupted over the Palestine conflict and over the new Anglo-Iraqi agreement, the Treaty of Portsmouth. The former were aimed at the large Jewish population in Baghdad, who soon concluded they had no future in Iraq and the vast majority of them left, leaving most of their property behind, in the early 1950s.[15] Nuri, now the dominant figure in Iraqi ruling circles, took the opportunity offered by the death of Abdullah I of Jordan to reclaim Iraqi leadership of schemes for unity in the Fertile Crescent. However, he now faced a rival to Iraqi regional leadership with the coming to power in 1952 of a new military regime in Egypt. By 1955, Colonel Gamal Abdul Nasser was the clear leader of the regime. Nasser's earliest achievement was to sign an agreement that ended British base rights in peacetime in Egypt. This contrasted with Nuri and the Iraqi royal family's continued advocacy of the British connection and the allowance of bases. Britain would retain air bases and military facilities and rights in Iraq until after the 1958 revolution.

Moreover, Nuri, influenced by a deep distrust of the Russians dating back to his days in the Ottoman army, was deeply committed to bringing Iraq firmly into the Western Alliance. To this end, in early 1955, he orchestrated the creation of a regional defence organisation, the Baghdad Pact, which included Britain, Iran, Turkey and Pakistan. Nuri eventually hoped to bring in other Arab states including Jordan and Syria into the alliance. The Baghdad Pact provoked fierce opposition from Nasser, who saw it as a challenge to his own preference for Arab states to be neutral in the Cold War and a block to his own ambitions for regional leadership.[16] The Egyptian leader directed the full weight of an increasingly powerful propaganda machine against the Iraqi leadership. Jordan decided not to join after Egyptian-inspired riots, and Syria became increasingly entranced by Nasser's brand of Arab nationalism. The Hashemites faced increasing isolation – a situation only exacerbated by the Anglo-French-Israeli invasion of Suez in October/November 1956.[17] An international crisis over Syria in the summer and autumn of 1957, in which, with British encouragement, Nuri floated a number of schemes for Iraqi intervention, only strengthened Egyptian influence. This influence culminated in a union of Egypt and Syria, called the United Arab Republic, under Nasser's leadership in February 1958. Nuri, in desperation, floated a counter-proposal – the Arab Union – made up of Iraq and Jordan, but it had little popular support.

Domestically the regime remained unstable. Iraq had huge social divisions between the peasant masses that saw little benefit from increased oil revenues and the landlord classes that grew ever more prosperous. The landed classes also excluded a growing middle class from the levers of power. A Development Board tasked with spending the oil revenues was the subject of criticism for moving too slowly. Nasserite propaganda over the Baghdad Pact tapped into widespread political disquiet about Iraq's pro-Western foreign policy.[18] The government treated even mild political opposition as subversion, leaving little opportunity for legitimate political opposition.[19]

Within the army the wider political discontent was reflected in the growth of groups in the officer class modelled on the Egyptian Free Officers. They became increasingly determined to end the regime. The opportunity arose in July 1958, when Iraqi troops were ordered to Jordan to bolster the regime there. Instead they marched on Baghdad and seized power. In appalling scenes, the royal family, including the youthful King and the former regent Abdullah, were slain. Nuri was captured attempting to reach a friendly foreign embassy, allegedly disguised in women's clothes, and murdered. Iraq was proclaimed a republic under Brigadier General Abd al-Karim Qasim (1914–63).

The 50 years since the fall of the Hashemites have been an undoubted disaster for Iraq. A series of brutal dictatorships have ruled the country culminating in the disastrous rule of Saddam Hussein from 1979. He presided over a debilitating war with Iran (1980–8), and an invasion and brutal occupation of Kuwait (1990–1) which led to war with an American-dominated military coalition, which destroyed Iraq's army. After the 9/11 attacks of 2001 by al-Qaeda, the United States decided to remove Saddam Hussein. While his regime was swiftly removed in the spring of 2003, the ensuing years have seen a violent insurgency and widespread destruction. Hundreds of thousands of Iraqis have died in the conflict.

If the Hashemites and their advisers such as Nuri had pursued a more vigorous reform agenda perhaps things might have worked out better. It is hard to see how they could have been much worse. The fractured sectarian nature of Iraq would always have been a problem for any regime but a more open polity might have mitigated matters. It says little for Republican Iraq that the 2005 elections were the first since 1953.[20]

Syria and Lebanon: from Mandate to independence

France maintained tight control of its Middle Eastern Mandates but faced continuous and often violent nationalist opposition especially in Syria. The ending of Ottoman rule in 1918 and the brief experiment with independence under Feisal's kingdom had provided an enormous boost to nationalism in Syria and nationalist parties, clubs and secret societies flourished.

The French had a wide range of conflicting political, cultural and economic goals in their Middle Eastern Mandates and tried various schemes to both satisfy and defang nationalism. France wanted to exploit Syria and the Lebanon economically, but was never able to make the Mandates pay for themselves. There was also the traditional French colonial goal of assimilation in evidence, i.e. to make Syria and the Lebanon a Francophone bridgehead in the Middle East, and to this end the French government supported and expanded its long-established educational and missionary organisations. This was strongly advocated by the small group of French politicians committed to the colonial project. However, the conditions of the Mandate, which emphasised the obligations of the Mandatory Power to guide its subjects to eventual independence (though without specifying a timescale), precluded settlement.

France rejected the solution of the British in Iraq and Transjordan, which was to hand over most powers to a native administration as soon as practicable and regulate their relationship by means of treaty. Instead, the French put in place an elaborate administrative infrastructure modelled on their existing arrangement in Morocco. Two Higher Commissioners, one for the Lebanon and one for Syria respectively, held overall control. A network of officials and army officers acted as advisers to local notables and collaborators who were given posts. As well as the division of the Lebanon and Syria, a federal system of small states was put in place, which it was hoped would encourage the widespread fissiparous tendencies within Syria's diverse religious and ethnic make-up. The federal strategy never really worked and nationalism remained a potent force. Only the Lebanon and the area around Alexandretta, which Turkey wanted back and which would eventually be returned to her in 1939, were able to permanently exclude themselves from Syria. The two major states of Syria, centred on Aleppo and Damascus, demanded reunification in 1924 and the French acquiesced. Smaller states based on Muslim religious minorities such as the Druze and Alawi lasted until 1936 before the French agreed to reincorporate them into Syria.

Nationalist resistance was never far from the surface. The most important political figures in Syria tended to be the urban Notables, wealthy absentee landowners and their families who lived in the major cities. They were generally nationalist in terms of their politics and many had aligned themselves with Feisal in 1919–20. These Notables dominated Syrian politics until the radical Arab nationalist Baath Party seized power in the 1960s. Some Notables, lured by the promise of office, were willing to collaborate with the French. The French also created a large locally recruited paramilitary force, *les Troupes Spéciales de Levant*. Its loyalty was ensured by a substantial proportion of the officer corps being French and by recruiting predominantly from the Christian and Shia minorities who had most to fear from a nationalist movement that was overwhelmingly Sunni.

The most violent attempt to overthrow French rule broke out in 1925 with a major rebellion by tribesmen from the

Druze Muslim sect.[21] This rebellion, popularly known as the 'Great Revolt', was 'a popular and widespread anti-imperialist uprising with a pronounced nationalist orientation'.[22] Laverty Miller argues that 'the revolution of 1925 was not the nationalist revolt of a united people against a French oppressor but a power struggle among and within divisive groups in an artificial state who could agree on only one thing: the French must go'.[23] Therefore, while the revolt was widespread, factionalism and ethnic divisions made it very difficult to create the single national grouping that might have forced the French to consider giving up their Mandate. Also, it was by no means universally supported. Some of the ethnic and religious minorities in Syria, especially the Christians, calculated that they had much to lose by an Arab nationalist takeover and the French were, in the end, able to prevail. However, it was not completely crushed until 1927. France's international reputation was seriously damaged by the decision to shell Damascus when rebels infiltrated the city in October 1925. This left much of the city in ruins.[24]

The defeat of the revolt convinced many Syrian nationalists that an uprising to drive the French out had no chance of success and that a gradual French withdrawal was the only way to advance Arab claims for independence. At the same time, the French realised that they could only rule Syria at an acceptable cost if they put in place structures that would give the nationalists some access to the levers of power. An alliance of nationalists, primarily from the ranks of the notables, formed the National Bloc. Their aim was to take advantage of the French programme of liberalisation, achieve positions in the governmental structure and accelerate moves towards independence.

The National Bloc controlled the Constituent Assembly

between 1928 and 1930. However, the French rejected the constitutional proposals of the Bloc, which called for virtual independence, abolished the Assembly and attempted to impose their own constitutional structures thereafter. However, the National Bloc was able to prevent Syrian agreement to any constitution which would be acceptable to the French. Despite this, the Bloc was moderate in its opposition to French rule. It kept channels open with the French High Commissioner and served in the various cabinets that the French established. The Bloc's willingness to collaborate undermined its influence with more radical nationalist groupings. Youth movements, mainly made up of students, began to grow in influence. Secret societies, the most notable being the Arab Liberation Society (established 1929) and the League of National Action, which superseded it from 1933, sprang up. These secret societies radicalised demonstrations in early 1936, which grew into a general strike. These demonstrations propitiously took place just before the left-wing Popular Front government assumed power in France. The Popular Front rapidly agreed a treaty broadly acceptable to Syrian opinion in September 1936. Entitled the Franco-Syrian Treaty of Friendship, it provided for France to grant independence and defend Syria in return for the use of military bases during international conflicts. It was agreed by the Syrian Parliament in December 1936. At the same time, the Lebanon was fully acknowledged as a separate and independent state, on much the same terms, under a parallel treaty.

However, a combination of the disintegration of the left-wing Popular Front government in Paris, nationalist faction-fighting, objections from frightened minorities and the handover of Alexandretta to Turkey ensured that the Treaty was never properly ratified. The more right-leaning

French governments of the late 1930s, concerned with the rise of Hitler, sought to put the independence process for their Middle Eastern Mandates on the backburner. Deadlock now ensued with Syrian nationalists demanding the French fulfil their part of the bargain. Violent Syrian objections to the return of Alexandretta to Turkey led to French direct rule being reimposed in 1939. The startling and unexpected defeat of France in May/June 1940 and the assumption of power of the Vichy regime, prepared to collaborate with Nazi Germany and Fascist Italy, gave both Axis Powers increased influence in Syria. The British, fearing an Axis assault on the Middle East, invaded Syria from Palestine and expelled the Vichy-imposed administration in June 1941. The Free French under General Charles de Gaulle promised independence subject to the conclusion of an acceptable treaty, but France's power in Syria and the Lebanon was in tatters. Britain and the United States now wielded increasing and decisive influence and they saw little gain for the West in the continuation of French rule. In 1943, the nationalists won elections called by the Free French administration under huge pressure from the British and the United States. Shukri al-Quwwatli, a radical pan-Arab, became President. France still controlled the *les Troupes Spéciales*, whom they used to try to prevent independence until French interests were guaranteed. France's refusal to withdraw culminated in May 1945 in the outbreak of anti-French riots. French attempts to restore order and their control were strongly criticised by the British who demanded France withdraw its forces. Bowing to international pressure, France finally conceded defeat and withdrew its forces in April 1946.[25]

Syria's experience of independence would not be an altogether happy one. From 1946 onwards, a series of unstable civilian and military governments held power. It also became a battleground from the mid-1950s between the desires of the Hashemite Kingdoms of Iraq and Jordan who were anxious to bring it into a Federation of the Fertile Crescent and the pan-Arab ambitions of President Nasser of Egypt. Nasser prevailed in this conflict and an Egyptian Syrian Union called the United Arab Republic was proclaimed in 1958.[26] Even this did not bring stability to Syria. In September 1961, there was a coup and the union with Egypt was severed. Army officers linked to the radical pan-Arab Baath Party seized power in March 1963. This extremely radical regime confronted Israel over water rights on the River Jordan. This contributed to the tension that led to the June 1967 Six-Day War in which Israel defeated Egypt, Jordan and Syria. The strategically important Golan Heights were lost to Israel. In 1970, after years of political infighting, General Hafez al-Assad became undisputed ruler of Syria. He led the country to war with Israel in coalition with Egypt in October 1973 but failed to regain the Golan Heights, which to this day remain under Israeli occupation.

The Lebanon's experience of independence would be no less troubled. The French arrested much of the Lebanese government after elections in 1943 brought anti-French groups to power. As in Syria, this was a forlorn attempt to maintain control and the British forced the French to retreat. In 1946, France withdrew its forces and the Lebanon became independent. However, gaining independence was only part of the Lebanon's political problems. The Lebanon's population was divided virtually 50–50 between various Christians sects (the most significant being Maronite Christians) and Muslims. Muslims were again split between Sunnis, Shias and a substantial Druze minority. Muslims were generally sympathetic to union with Syria. An unwritten grand political compromise, called the National Pact, was agreed between the Christian leaders and Muslims in 1943. This provided for a permanent division of political spoils between Christians, who received the Presidency in perpetuity and Muslims who were guaranteed the office of Prime Minister. A ratio of six Christians to five Muslim members of parliament was also enshrined. The Christians compromised by accepting that the Lebanon would be an Arab state.

Until the 1970s, the Lebanon was the financial centre of the Middle East and appeared to be the most successful of the Arab states. However, beneath the surface of calm and prosperity lay substantial communal tensions. The Lebanon also found itself drawn into the inter-Arab disputes of the 1950s, the Israel-Palestine conflict due to the sizeable population of Palestinian refugees, as well as the wider world struggle between the United States and the Soviet Union. The Lebanon's National Pact held until the late 1950s when the tensions caused by the intra-Arab struggle and the growing internal troubles of a divided communal society, led to a brief civil war. From the late 1960s Lebanese-based Palestinian guerrilla attacks on Israel provoked ever greater Israeli reprisals that destabilised relations between the Christian and Muslim communities. In 1975, full-scale fighting broke out between Christians and Palestinians, which widened into a 15-year Muslim-Christian civil war.

President Assad of Syria intervened militarily in the Lebanon constantly from 1975 until the end of the Civil War in 1990.[27] Despite a heavy defeat by Israel in south Lebanon in 1982, Assad was able to successfully use Shia militia, most notably the radical Hezbollah, to force an Israeli withdrawal, humiliate a United States military force and eventually rout the anti-Syrian Christian factions. The end of the war in 1990 entrenched Syria's special position in the Lebanon. The Lebanon began a slow recovery, punctuated by ferocious Israeli military reactions to terrorist attacks on its security zone in the south and in Israel proper. The withdrawal of Israeli forces in 2000 promised peace but in 2006 there was a vicious but inconclusive war between Israel and the Hezbollah.

Conclusion

Malcolm Yapp, one of the leading historians of the modern Middle East, complains that the 'history of the modern Near East has often been written as though the states were driftwood in the sea of international affairs, their destinies shaped by the decisions of others'.[1] Certainly many historians, as well as the indigenous population of the region, subscribe to the notion that the Middle East is a plaything of the Great Powers. There is therefore a tendency to ignore equally, if not more, crucial influences such as shifting demographics, battles within indigenous elites and economic factors. However, it is easy to see why the settlement in the aftermath of the First World War is viewed by many historians and Arab nationalists as a *diktat* imposed by the outside Powers. Furthermore, since the boundaries established in 1919–25 for the Mandates have proved remarkably durable, it is understandable that many Arab nationalist critics view the system of states that grew out of the Mandates as artificial and alien.

However, there is a counter view to this which points to the fact that the local forces in the Middle East are often the conduits for bringing in external forces. This is where the Hashemites are important. To their critics and even some friendly observers, they were opportunists, with hardly an Arab nationalist bone in their body. Nonetheless, they had a remarkable ability to use the First World War for their own purposes, which partially chimed with the emerging Arab nationalist cause. Moreover, they were not alone in doing this. Czech, Irish and Polish nationalists were able to use the factors created by the War to forge new nations. These may have had a more sophisticated ideology of nationalism than the Hashemites but there is little evidence to suggest that these advanced nationalists would have succeeded without the funeral pyre of empires that was the First World War. Even if they were not sophisticated nationalists in the European sense, the Hashemites were important elements in forging the founding myths of Arab nationalism. The phrase 'founding myths' is not used here in a pejorative sense. All nations are, to an extent, founded on myth. However, the emergence of modern Arab nationalism in the first 25 years of the 20th century is more exposed to the charge of being based on myth than most because it has the disadvantage of being relatively recent and documented in great detail. This massive weight of documentation is overwhelmingly written by outsiders. While some is sympathetic, much is not. It is difficult to find the authentic voice of the Arabs among it.

Criticism of the Peace settlement in the Middle East rests mainly on the point that it prevented the emergence of an Arab nation that would have been able to hold its own in the world. If a state encompassing all the Arab areas of the Middle East and Egypt had been allowed to emerge under Hashemite or other leadership, its potential would have been enormous. In land area it would have been the second biggest in the world after Russia. It would have contained at the end of the 20th century a population second only to that of

China. Nearly two-thirds of the world's oil reserves would have lain within its territory, and the money generated by oil production would have facilitated transfers between the oil-rich and the oil-deficient regions, providing capital for economic development. As one commentator noted, it 'is easy to comprehend why this dream has long intoxicated Arab nationalists'.[2]

The argument of Arab nationalists that unity was prevented by foreign powers has been strenuously challenged. This viewpoint suggests that if the Arab Middle East had been left to its own devices in the aftermath of the collapse of the Ottoman Empire, it would have broken down into warring tribes and factions and it is highly unlikely that one individual or group would have been able to forge an Arab nation. The struggle between Ibn Saud and Hussein for dominance in the Arabian Peninsula, which was mainly carried out with little intervention from the Western Powers, suggests that a period of internecine fighting may well have followed the War throughout the entire Middle East if the Arabs had been left to their own devices.

How should history judge the Hashemites? It is clear that they should be judged as successful opportunists. There is no doubt that they did not get what they thought they were promised by the British. However, two kingdoms was a not insubstantial gain for a family whose influence at the start of the War scarcely extended much beyond Mecca. A third kingdom might have survived if Hussein had maintained his alliance with the British. Furthermore, the Hashemite Kingdoms that did emerge in Iraq and Transjordan were ruled reasonably effectively. It would be a travesty of history to suggest that the Hashemites were democrats or did much to alleviate the appalling social injustices in these countries, but their inheritance, particularly in Transjordan, was a poor, desperately under-resourced one. Abdullah and his grandson, King Hussein, did remarkably well to preserve it without descending to the depths of brutality indulged in by the secular Arab nationalist regimes that emerged in surrounding states which claimed to represent the popular will. In Iraq, the Hashemites, while they formally ruled from 1921 to 1958, were unlucky that Feisal died prematurely in 1933. His successors were far too young to take over the reins of power. As a consequence, there was considerable political instability in Iraq from that point on. Even then, while to suggest that Iraq was a functioning democratic, constitutional democracy would be far from the truth, it was a relative paradise of free expression in comparison to what emerged in the years after the fall of the monarchy in 1958 and efforts to develop the economy with oil money were beginning. The Hashemites' principal difficulty in Iraq was that they were Sunni rulers in a country that was majority Shia. One of their unfortunate legacies was that the template of a small Sunni ruling class that they established was perpetuated and indeed worsened by their republican successors.

The British and French governments do not emerge particularly well from the peace settlement in the Middle East. Decisions taken, from the Sykes-Picot Agreement in 1916 to the Mandate system announced at San Remo, took far too much account of the needs of the Great Powers at the expense of the Arabs. France emerges particularly badly. Its rule in Syria from 1920 was characterised by considerable indifference to the wishes of the population. With the Sherifian Solution, imperfect that it was, the British showed a capacity to develop policies that at least allowed for political growth and development. These policies may have emerged from a need to cut military costs in the Middle East but nonetheless did allow a reasonable degree of independence to emerge for Iraq within a decade. However, British bases and influence remained under treaties unfavourable to the local states. This continued British political and military influence brought one major benefit. It helped preserve the Middle East from Axis invasion during the Second World War. Britain and its allies were able to use the Middle East as a major base to launch campaigns that significantly contributed to Allied victory. The presence of these bases in Iraq but more especially in Egypt would be a source of tension between Arab nationalists and Britain in the post-war period. The major British problems in the Middle East were in Palestine. Arab nationalists everywhere were offended by her on-off commitment to the Balfour Declaration's proposal for a homeland for Jews there. The legacy of the Balfour Declaration would cause no end of trouble.

It is widely acknowledged that the Paris Peace Conference and the treaties that emerged from it were a failure. They utterly failed in their primary objective to remove the causes of war. They failed because the remedies put forward by the peacemakers – reparations, national self-determination, disarmament, Mandates and the League of Nations – were either wrong or not implemented properly. Considering the catalogue of disasters that emerged from the peace settlement – the failure to contain Germany, the creation of failed states such as Yugoslavia and the unhappy birth of the modern Middle East – it is difficult to single one out as being the greatest failure. However, as the German and to lesser extent, Yugoslav questions have been largely resolved after appalling wars, the continuing Middle Eastern crisis can certainly lay claim to being the longest-lasting unfinished legacy of the Paris Peace Conference.

Notes

Preface

1. William Orpen, *An Onlooker in France 1917–1919* (Williams & Norgate, London: 1924) p 105.
2. See for instance Gertrude Bell to her father 31 July 1921. Her correspondence can be read at *www.gerty.ncl.ac.uk*
3. Stephen Bonsal. *Suitors and Suppliants: The Little Nations at Versailles*. (Prentice-Hall, Inc, New York: 1946) p 50.
4. David Fromkin, *A Peace to End All Peace: The Fall of the Ottoman Empire and the Creation of the Modern Middle East* (Phoenix, London: 2000.) p 346.
5. Bonsal, *Suitors and Suppliants*, p 52.
6. Jeremy Wilson, *Lawrence of Arabia: The Authorized Biography of T E Lawrence* (Atheneum, New York: 1990) p 581.

1 The Arab World and the Hashemites before the First World War

1. C Ernest Dawn, 'From Ottomanism to Arabism: The Origin of an Ideology', *The Review of Politics*, Vol 23, No 3 (Jul 1961) p 378.

2. English Arabist, traveller and diplomat, Gertrude Bell, cited in David Fromkin, *A Peace to End All Peace* (Deutsch, London: 1989) p 35.

3. Ira Lapidus, *A History of Islamic Societies* (Cambridge University Press, Cambridge: 2002) p 535.

4. As characterised in Albert Hourani, 'Ottoman Reform and the Politics of Notables', in William R Polk and Richard L Chambers (eds), *Beginnings of Modernisation the Middle East: The Nineteenth Century* (University of Chicago Press, Chicago: 1968) pp 41–68.

5. James L Gelvin, *Divided Loyalties: Nationalism and Mass Politics in Syria at the Close of Empire* (University of California Press, Berkeley: 1998) p 13.

6. M E Yapp, *The Making of the Modern Near East, 1792–1923* (Longman, Harlow: 1987) pp 132–3.

7. Dawn, 'From Ottomanism to Arabism,' p 10–11.

8. Amongst critical looks at Antonius are Sylvia G Haim, '"The Arab Awakening", A Source for the Historian?', *Die Welt des Islams*, II (1953); Elie Kedourie, *England and the Middle East: The Destruction of the Ottoman Empire, 1914–1921* (London, Boulder: 1987) pp 29–66 and 107–41; Elie Kedourie, *In the Anglo-Arab Labyrinth: The McMahon-Husayn Correspondence and Its Interpretations 1914–1939* (Cambridge University Press, Cambridge: 1976) pp 64–136 and 266–9; Albert Hourani, '"*The Arab Awakening*," Forty Years Later', in Derek Hopwood (ed), *Studies in Arab History: The Antonius Lectures, 1978–87* (Macmillan, Basingstoke: 1990) pp 21–40.

9. Hourani, '"*The Arab Awakening*" Forty Years Later', p 26.

10. George Antonius, *The Arab Awakening* (Putnam, New York: 1946) pp 37, 80, 81; Zeine N Zeine, *Arab Turkish Relations and the Emergence of Arab Nationalism* (Khayat's, Beirut: 1958) pp 56, 57, 68.

11. S S Boyle, *Betrayal in Palestine: the story of George Antonius* (Westview Press, Boulder, Colo: 2001) and the more venerable Antonius, *The Arab Awakening*, for further details on Antonius.

12. See C Ernest Dawn, 'The Origins of Arab Nationalism', in Rashid Khalidi *et al* (eds), *The Origins of Arab Nationalism* (Columbia University Press, New York: 1991) pp 18–19.

13. Eliezer Tauber, *The Emergence of the Arab Movements* (Frank Cass, London: 1993) p 406. Ernest Dawn, *From Ottomanism to Arabism: Essays on the Origins of Arab Nationalism* (University of Illinois Press, Urbana: 1973) pp 152–3 puts the figure at only 144.

14. Most notably Efraim Karsh and Inari Karsh, *Empires of the Sand: The Struggle for Mastery in the Middle East, 1789–1923* (Harvard University Press, Cambridge MA: 1999) are very hostile to what they consider the imperialist ambitions of Sherif Hussein and the Hashemites.

15. A useful summation of Dawn's more than three decades of musing on the subject is in Dawn, 'The Origins of Arab Nationalism', in Khalidi *et al* (eds), *The Origins of Arab Nationalism,* pp 3–31.

16. Majid Khadduri, *Political Trends in the Arab World: The Role of Ideas and Ideals in Politics* (John Hopkins Press, Baltimore: 1970) p 19.

17. Quoted in Martin Kramer, *Arab Awakening and Islamic Revival: The Politics of Ideas in the Middle East* (Transaction Publishers, New Brunswick: 1996) p 24.

18. Raymond A Hinnebusch, *Authoritarian Power and State Formation in Ba'thist Syria: Army, Party, and Peasant* (Westview Press, Boulder, Colo: 1990) p 45.

19. W Ochsenwald, *Religion, Society and the State in Arabia: The Hijaz under Ottoman Control 1840–1908* (Ohio State University Press, Columbus OH: 1984) p 17.

20. Ochsenwald, *Religion, Society and the State in Arabia*, p 220.

21. W Ochsenwald, 'Ironic origins: Arab nationalism in the Hijaz', in Rashid Khalidi *et al* (eds), *The Origins of Arab Nationalism* (Columbia University Press, New York: 1991) p 190.

22. James Morris, *The Hashemite Kings* (Faber and Faber, London: 1959) p 18.

23. Kedourie, *In the Anglo-Arab Labyrinth*, p 11.

24. Cited in Tufan Buzpinar, 'Opposition to the Ottoman Caliphate in the Early Years of Abdülhamid II: 1877–1882', *Die Welt des Islams*, New Ser Vol 36, Issue 1 (Mar 1996), p 67.

25. See Elizabeth Monroe, *Britain's Moment in the Middle East 1914–1956* (Methuen, London: 1963) pp 11–23.

26. Cited in Buzpinar, 'Opposition to the Ottoman Caliphate in the Early Years of Abdülhamid II', p 80.

27. What follows is substantially based on R Baker, *King Husain and the Kingdom of Hejaz* (Oleander Press, Cambridge: 1979); Kedourie, *In the Anglo-Arab labyrinth*; A Susser and A Shmuelevitz (eds), *The Hashemites in the Modern Arab World: Essays in Honour of the Late Professor Uriel Dann* (Frank

Cass, London: 1995); Morris, *The Hashemite Kings*; Joshua Teitelbaum, *The Rise and Fall of the Hashemite Kingdom of Arabia* (Hurst, London: 2001); and Haifa Alangaria, *The Struggle for Power in Arabia: Ibn Saud, Hussein and Great Britain, 1914–1924* (Ithaca Press, Reading: 1998).

28. Morris, *The Hashemite Kings*, p 23.
29. T E Lawrence, *Seven Pillars of Wisdom* (Wordsworth, London: 1997) p 84.
30. Lawrence, *Seven Pillars of Wisdom*, p 86.
31. Morris, *The Hashemite Kings*, pp 24–5.
32. Teitelbaum, *The Rise and Fall of the Hashemite Kingdom of Arabia*, p 41.
33. Teitelbaum, *The Rise and Fall of the Hashemite Kingdom of Arabia*, p 41.
34. Abdullah, *Memoirs of King Abdullah of Transjordan* (Cape, London: 1950) p 70.
35. J Nevo, 'Abdullah's memoirs as historical source material', in A Susser and A Shmuelevitz, *The Hashemites in the Modern Arab World: Essays in Honour of the Late Professor Uriel Dann* (Frank Cass, London: 1995) p 166.
36. Sir Louis Mallet to Sir Edward Grey, 18 March 1914, reproduced in G P Gooch and Harold Temperley, *British Documents on the Origins of the War, 1898–1914*, Vol X, Part II (H.M.S.O., London: 1938) p 827, hereafter *British Docs*.
37. Alangaria, *The Struggle for Power in Arabia*, p 63.
38. See James Nicholson, 'The Hejaz railway', *Asian Affairs*, 37:3 (2006) pp 320–36 for the story of the railway.
39. Teitelbaum, *The Rise and Fall of the Hashemite Kingdom of Arabia*, p 69.

40. Teitelbaum, *The Rise and Fall of the Hashemite Kingdom of Arabia*, pp 69–70.
41. A I Dawisha, *Arab Nationalism in the Twentieth Century: From Triumph to Despair* (Princeton University Press, Princeton: 2003) p 35.
42. See Oschenwald, 'Ironic Origins: Arab Nationalism in the Hijaz', pp 189–203.

2 The First World War and the Rise of Arab Nationalism

1. Ulrich Trumpener, *Germany and the Ottoman Empire 1914–1918* (Princeton University Press, Princeton: 1968) pp 70–1.
2. M S Anderson, *The Eastern Question, 1774–1923* (Macmillan, London: 1966) p 260.
3. See Marian Kent, 'Great Britain and the End of the Ottoman Empire, 1900–23' in Marian Kent (ed), *The Great Powers and the End of the Ottoman Empire* (G. Allen & Unwin, London: 1984) pp 173–85 for an account of British pre-war policy towards the Ottomans.
4. Cited in Hew Strachan, *The First World War*: Vol. 1 *To Arms* (Oxford University Press, Oxford: 2001) p 696.
5. Lord Kitchener to Sir Edward Grey, 6/2/1914 reproduced in *British Docs*, Vol X, p 827. See also Kedourie, *In the Anglo-Arab Labyrinth*, p 5.
6. Kitchener to Gray, 14/2/1914 *British Docs*, Vol X, p 827.
7. Kedourie, *In the Anglo-Arab Labyrinth*, p 7
8. C Ernest Dawn, 'The Amir of Mecca Al-Husayn Ibn-'Ali and the Origin of the Arab Revolt', *Proceedings of the American Philosophical Society*, Vol 104, No 1 (15 Feb 1960) p 22; Kedourie, *England and the Middle East*, pp 19, 52.

9. Kedourie, *In the Anglo-Arab Labyrinth*, pp 21–2.

10. Joshua Teitelbaum, 'Sherif Hussein ibn Ali and the Hashemite vision of the post-Ottoman order: from chieftaincy to suzerainty', *Middle Eastern Studies*, 34:1 (1998) p 106.

11. Kedourie, *In the Anglo-Arab Labyrinth*, pp 20–5.

12. For a more detailed discussion of British policy see Jukka Nevakivi, *Britain, France, and the Middle East, 1914–1920* (Athlone Press, London: 1969) Chapter 2.

13. Kedourie, *In the Anglo-Arab Labyrinth*, Chapter 2; Monroe, *Britain's Moment in the Middle East*, Chapter 1; and Isaiah Friedman, *The Question of Palestine, 1914–1918; British-Jewish-Arab Relations* (Schocken Books, New York: 1973) Chapter 2.

14. Kitchener's paper is quoted in Nevakivi, *Britain, France, and the Middle East*, p 18. Asquith is quoted in p 17.

15. The paper entitled 'British Desiderate in Turkey and Asia: Report, Proceedings and Appendices of a Committee Appointed by the Prime Minister, 1915', PRO CAB 27/1, pp 3–29 is substantively reproduced as Doc. 12 in J C Hurewitz, *The Middle East and North Africa in World Politics* 2 (Yale University Press, New Haven: 1979) pp 26–45.

16. Kedourie, *England and the Middle East*, pp 48–56.

17. Dawn, 'Ottomanism to Arabism', p 28.

18. Antonius, *The Arab Awakening*, p 79.

19. Fromkin, *A Peace to End All Peace*, pp 174–6.

20. Dawn, 'The Amir of Mecca Al-Husayn Ibn-'Ali and the Origin of the Arab Revolt', p 24.

21. T E Lawrence, report, 13 May 1917, NOTES ON HEJAZ AFFAIRS *Arab Bulletin* (13 May 1917).

22. Mary C Wilson, 'The Hashemites, the Arab Revolt, and Arab Nationalism', in Rashid Khalidi *et al* (eds), *The Origins of Arab Nationalism* (Columbia University Press, New York: 1991) p 214.

23. Efraim Karsh and Inari Karsh, 'Myth in the Desert, or not the Great Arab Revolt', *Middle Eastern Studies* 33:2 (1997) p 267.

3 Negotiating for an Arab State

1. Amir Abdullah to Ronald Storrs, 14 July 1915. The correspondence can be found in Great Britain, *Parliamentary Papers,* 1939, Misc. no 3. Cmd 5957.

2. Ronald Storrs, *Orientations* (I. Nicholson & Watson, London: 1939) pp 160–1.

3. The correspondence can be found in Great Britain, *Parliamentary Papers,* 1939 Misc. no 3, Cmd. 5957 or in Antonius, *The Arab Awakening*, Chapter 6.

4. The following draws on Kedourie, *In the Anglo-Arab Labyrinth*, Chapter 2, Monroe, *Britain's Moment in the Middle East*, Chapter 2, Friedman, *The Question of Palestine*, Chapter 6, and Briton Cooper Busch, *Britain, India and the Arabs, 1914–1921* (University of California Press, Berkeley: 1971) Chapter 2.

5. Kedourie, *In the Anglo-Arab Labyrinth*, p 4.

6. Kedourie, *In the Anglo-Arab Labyrinth*, p 120.

7. From Sherif Hussein to McMahon, 9 September 1915 in Cmd. 5957.

8. Fromkin, *A Peace to End All Peace*, pp 176–80.

9. Friedman, *The Question of Palestine*, p 72.

10. Fromkin, *A Peace to End All Peace*, pp 177–8.

11. Kedourie, *England and Middle East*, Chapter 2; Monroe, *Britain's Moment in the Middle East*,

4. Howard Morley Sachar, *The Emergence of the Middle East, 1914–1924* (Allen Lane, The Penguin Press, London: 1970) pp 134–5.

5. Westrate, *The Arab Bureau*, pp 6–9.

6. T E Lawrence to Lord Curzon 27 September 1919 in David Garnett (ed), *The Letters of T E Lawrence* (Jonathan Cape, London: 1938) pp 291–3.

7. The best biographies are Lawrence James, *The Golden Warrior: the Life and Legend of Lawrence of Arabia*, rev. edn (Abacus, London: 1996); and Jeremy Wilson, *Lawrence of Arabia: The Authorised Biography of T E Lawrence* (Heinemann, London: 1989).

8. R. Aldington, *Lawrence of Arabia: A Biographical Enquiry* (Collins, London: 1955).

9. Lawrence, *Seven Pillars of Wisdom*, p 76.

10. See Lawrence, *Seven Pillars of Wisdom*, p 51, which questions Abdullah's sincerity.

11. James Barr, *Setting the Desert on Fire: T E Lawrence and Britain's Secret War in Arabia, 1916–18* (Bloomsbury, London: 2007) pp 102–3.

12. Lawrence, *Seven Pillars of Wisdom*, pp 183–4.

13. Lawrence, *Seven Pillars of Wisdom*, p 215.

14. Lawrence, *Seven Pillars of Wisdom*, p 85.

15. Robert Lansing, *The Big Four and Others of the Peace Conference* (Houghton Mifflin Company, Boston: 1921) pp 163–5.

16. Wilson, *Lawrence of Arabia*, pp 361–2.

17. Two recent accounts of Lawrence and the Arab Revolt are Barr, *Setting the Desert on Fire*, and Wilson, *Lawrence of Arabia*, Chapters 13–26.

18. See Helmut Mejcher, 'British Middle East Policy 1917–21: The Inter-Departmental Level', *Journal*

of Contemporary History, Vol 8, No 4 (Oct 1973) pp 81–101.

19. Fromkin, *A Peace to End All Peace*, pp 292–4.

20. Tom Segev, *One Palestine Complete* (John Murray, London: 2001).

21. Leonard Stein, *The Balfour Declaration* (Simon and Schuster, New York: 1961); Mayir Vereti, 'The Balfour Declaration and its Makers', *Middle Eastern Studies*, vi (1970) pp 48–76; Friedman, *The Question of Palestine*; Ronald Sanders, *The High Walls of Jerusalem: A History of the Balfour Declaration and the Birth of the British Mandate for Palestine* (Holt, Reinhart and Winston, New York: 1983); David Vital, *Zionism: The Crucial Phase* (Clarendon Press, Oxford: 1987); and Fromkin, *A Peace to End All Peace*, Chapters 31–35.

22. See Mark Levene, 'The Balfour Declaration: A Case of Mistaken Identity', *The English Historical Review*, Vol 107, No 422 (Jan 1992) pp 54–77.

23. Antonius, *The Arab Awakening*, p 269.

24. Kedourie, *In the Anglo-Arab Labyrinth*, pp 190–1.

25. Friedman, *Question of Palestine*, p 328.

26. Fromkin, *A Peace to End all Peace*, pp 288–9.

27. Teitelbaum, 'Sherif Husayn ibn Ali and the Hashemite vision of the post-Ottoman order', p 109.

28. Lawrence, *Seven Pillars of Wisdom*, p 551.

29. Wilson, *Lawrence of Arabia*, pp 469–70, 511–12.

30. Kedourie, *England and the Middle East*, p 122.

31. Wilson, *Lawrence of Arabia*, p 566.

32. See Wilson, *Lawrence of Arabia*, pp 566–8.

33. TNA UK, CAB 23181482, War Cabinet Meeting, 3 October 1918.

34. Fromkin, *A Peace to End All Peace*, pp 338–9.

35. See John Fisher, 'Syria and Mesopotamia in British Middle Eastern Policy in 1919', *Middle Eastern Studies* 34:2 (Apr 1998) p 130.

36. Fisher, 'Syria and Mesopotamia', p 131.

37. Meir Zamir, 'Faisal and the Lebanese Question, 1918–20', *Middle Eastern Studies* 27:3 (Jul 1991) pp 404–26.

38. Zeine N Zeine, *The Struggle for Arab Independence: Western Diplomacy and the Rise and Fall of Faisal's Kingdom in Syria* (Khayats, Beirut: 1960) p 33.

39. Zeine, *The Struggle for Arab Independence*, pp 213–14.

40. See Gelvin, *Divided Loyalties*, pp 27–8.

41. Anderson, *The Eastern Question*, p 378.

42. Fromkin, *A Peace to End All Peace*, p 341.

43. The text is in Cmd. 5974, *Report of Committee set up to consider certain correspondence between Sir Henry McMahon and the Sherif of Mecca in 1915 and 1916*, pp 50–1.

44. Nevakivi, *Britain France, and the Arab Middle East*, p 82.

45. John Darwin, *Britain, Egypt and the Middle East: Imperial Policy in the Aftermath of War, 1918–1922* (Macmillan, London: 1981) p 155.

5 Feisal and the Peace Conference

1. Zeine, *The Struggle for Arab Independence*, pp 49–51.

2. Wilson, *Lawrence of Arabia*, p 586.

3. Kedourie, *In the Anglo-Arab Labyrinth*, p 213.

4. Timothy J Paris, 'British Middle East Policy-Making after the First World War: The Lawrentian and Wilsonian Schools', *The Historical Journal*, Vol 41, No 3 (Sep 1998) p 773.

5. See the discussions in Marian Kent, *Oil and Empire: British Policy and Mesopotamian Oil, 1900–1920* (Macmillan, London: 1976) pp 124–6, and Darwin, *Britain, Egypt and the Middle East*, pp 258–65.

6. There is no actual official government note of this conversation. See S W Roskill, *Hankey, Man of Secrets* Vol 2, 1919–1931 (Collins, London: 1972) pp 28–9. In August 1919 Clemenceau relied on the meeting to accuse Britain of perfidy in Doc 242 of DBFP I/4. See also Lloyd George, *The Truth about the Peace Treaties*, p 1038.

7. Wilson, *Lawrence of Arabia*, p 591.

8. Quoted in V H Rothwell, 'Mesopotamia in British War Aims, 1914–1918', *The Historical Journal*, Vol 13, No 2 (Jun 1970) p 287.

9. Paris, 'British Middle East Policy-Making after the First World War', p 779. See also Timothy J Paris, *Britain, the Hashemites, and Arab Rule, 1920–1925: The Sherifian Solution* (Frank Cass, London: 2003).

10. John Fisher, *Curzon and British Imperialism in the Middle East 1916–19* (Frank Cass, London: 1999) p xv.

11. Wilson, *Lawrence of Arabia*, pp 592–93.

12. Charles D Smith 'The Invention of a Tradition: The Question of Arab Acceptance of the Zionist Right to Palestine during World War I', *Journal of Palestine Studies*, XXII, 2 (Winter 1993) pp 56–7.

13. Diary of the Peace Conference Jan 1919, in Garnett (ed), *Letters of T E Lawrence*, pp 273–4.

14. Unless otherwise stated, this is based on *Papers Relating to the Foreign Relations of the United States, 1919: The Paris Peace Conference* (13 vols, Washington, D.C.: 1942–7) Vol 3 (1919) pp 889–94, hereafter *FRUS PPC (1919)*.

15. Sir James Headlam-Morley, *A Memoir of the Paris Peace Conference, 1919* (Methuen, London: 1972) pp 30–1.
16. Lloyd George, *The Truth about the Peace Treaties*, p 1038.
17. Stephen Bonsal, *Suitors and Supplicants: The Little Nations at Versailles* (Prentice-Hal inc, New York: 1946) p 32.
18. Bonsal, *Suitors and Supplicants*, p 33.
19. *FRUS PPC (1919)*, Vol. 3, pp 889–90.
20. *FRUS PPC (1919)*, Vol. 3, p 1016.
21. *FRUS PPC (1919)*, Vol. 3, pp 1024–38.
22. *FRUS PPC (1919)*, Vol. 3, p 1029.
23. *FRUS PPC (1919)*, Vol. 3, p 1030.
24. Meir Zamir, 'Faisal and the Lebanese Question, 1918–20,' *Middle Eastern Studies*, 27:3 (Jul 1991) p 408.
25. See M MacMillan, *Peacemakers: the Paris Peace Conference of 1919 and its attempt to end war* (Murray, London: 2001) p 402.
26. Bonsal, *Suitors and Supplicants*, p 45.
27. Lloyd George, *The Truth about the Peace Treaties*, pp 1048–9.
28. This meeting is described in Lloyd George, *The Truth about the Peace Treaties*, pp 1057–73 and *FRUS PPC (1919)*, Vol 5, pp 1–14.
29. Christopher M Andrew and Alexander Sydney Kanya-Forstner, *France Overseas: The Great War and the Climax of French Imperial Expansion* (Thames and Hudson, London, 1981) p 197.
30. *FRUS PPC (1919)*, Vol 7, p 747.
31. Notes of a conversation between Colonel House and Emir Feisal, 29 March 1919, in Garnett, *Letters of T E Lawrence*, p 275.

32. P Mantoux, *The Deliberations of the Council of Four, March 24-June 28, 1919. Notes of the Official Interpreter, Paul Mantoux. Vol. I: To the Delivery to the German Delegation of the Preliminaries of Peace. Vol. II: From the Delivery of the Peace Terms to the German Delegation to the Signing of the Treaty of Versailles* (Princeton University Press, Princeton, N.J.: 1992) Vol I, pp 41–57.

33. Tanenbaum, 'France and the Arab Middle East, 1914–1920', pp 29–30.

34. Colonel House Diary, 14/4/1919 in Woodrow Wilson and Arthur Stanley Link, *The Papers of Woodrow Wilson* (Princeton University Press, Princeton, N.J.: 1986–92) Vol 57, pp 334–5, hereafter *Wilson Papers*.

35. Westerman memo c. 17/4/1919 in *Wilson Papers*, Vol 57, p 444.

6 The Collapse of Feisal's Kingdom of Syria

1. E L Woodward and Rohan Butler, *Documents on British Foreign Policy 1919–39. First Series, Vol. IV, 1919, Chapter II Introductory note p 253,* hereafter refered to as *DBFP, First Series Vol. IV.* All further references to *DBFP* volumes are to Document Number not page number.

2. Doc 173, *DBFP, First Series Vol. IV.*

3. Doc 174, *DBFP, First Series Vol. IV.*

4. Doc 183, *DBFP, First Series, Vol. IV.*

5. TNA Fo14I158 119130/3 Political Officer Baghdad to High Commissioner Egypt, 30 May 1919.

6. Doc 189, Annex B, *DBFP, First Series, Vol. IV.*

7. Doc 182, Enc. 1 *DBFP, First Series, Vol. IV.*

8. Doc 176, *DBFP, First Series, Vol. IV.*

9. James L Gelvin, 'The Ironic Legacy of the King-Crane Commission' in David W Lesch, *The Middle East and the United States: A Historical and Political Reassessment* (Westview Press, Boulder, Colo.: 1996) p 16.

10. Doc 181, *DBFP, First Series Vol. IV*.

11. Doc 192, *DBFP, First Series Vol. IV*.

12. Gelvin, 'The Ironic Legacy of the King-Crane Commission', p 16.

13. The full itinerary is in *FRUS PPC (1919)*, Vol 12, pp 753–4.

14. Doc 199 *DBFP, First Series Vol. IV*.

15. Gelvin, *Divided Loyalties*, p 35.

16. *Wilson Papers*, Vol 61, p 442.

17. *FRUS PPC (1919)*, Vol 12, p 749.

18. *FRUS PPC (1919)*, Vol 12, p 750.

19. Karsh and Karsh, *Empires of the Sand*, p 278.

20. See Doc 178 *DBFP, First Series Vol. IV*, and Karsh and Karsh, *Empires of the Sand*, p 279, who are critical of Feisal's illusions and the British role in encouraging them.

21. *FRUS PPC (1919)*, Vol 12, pp 787–97 for recommendations.

22. *Wilson Papers*, Vol 64, p 27.

23. Harry N Howard, *The King-Crane Commission: An American Inquiry in the Middle East* (Khayats, Beirut: 1963) p 258.

24. Darwin, *Britain, Egypt and the Middle East*, p 171.

25. Doc 242, *DBFP, First Series Vol. IV*.

26. Doc 236, *DBFP, First Series Vol. IV*.

27. Doc 256, *DBFP, First Series Vol. IV*.

28. Doc 265, *DBFP, First Series Vol. IV*.

29. Doc 278, *DBFP, First Series Vol. IV.*
30. Doc 283, *DBFP, First Series Vol. IV.*
31. Doc 295, *DBFP, First Series Vol. IV.*
32. Doc 334, *DBFP, First Series Vol. IV.*
33. Doc 383, *DBFP, First Series Vol. IV.*
34. Karsh and Karsh, *Empires of the Sand*, p 281; Sachar, *The Emergence of the Middle East*, pp 272–3.
35. Doc. 412, *DBFP, First Series Vol. IV.*
36. Gertrude Bell to Family 12 Oct 1919. Gertrude Bell's Diaries and letters have been digitized by the University of Newcastle and are available at http://www.gerty.ncl.ac.uk/.All references to Bell's Diaries and Letters are to that source.
37. Bell Diary, 8 Oct 1919.
38. G. Bell to Family, 12 Oct 1919.
39. Bell Diary, 13 Oct 1919.
40. TNA Fo371/ 4152: 'Syria in October 1919', Nov 1919.
41. Doc 12, *DBFP, First Series Vol. VII.*
42. Malcolm B Russell, *The First Modern Arab State: Syria Under Faysal, 1918–1920.* (Bibliotheca Islamica, Minneapolis: 1985) pp 166–8.
43. Doc 214 in Rohan Butler, J P T Bury and M A Lambert (eds), *Documents On British Foreign Policy, 1919–1939 – FIRST SERIES Volume XIII The Near and Middle East January 1920 – March 1921* (London: 1963) hereafter *DBFP First Series Vol. XIII.*
44. Doc 219, *DBFP First Series Vol. XIII.*
45. Doc 221, *DBFP First Series Vol. XIII.*
46. Martin Gilbert, *Winston S. Churchill, Vol. 4 – Jan 1917– March 1921; Companion documents, Part 2* (Houghton Mifflin Company, Boston MA: 1978) p 1050, hereafter

Churchill Companion IV, 1917–1922 and Docs 217, 223, 224, *DBFP First Series Vol.XIII.*

47. Russell, *The First Modern Arab State*, pp 138–9.
48. Russell, *The First Modern Arab State*, pp 142–6.
49. Doc 251, *DBFP First Series Vol. XIII.*
50. Dan Eldar, 'France in Syria: The Abolition of the Sharifian Government, April-July 1920', *Middle Eastern Studies* 29:3 (Jul 1993) pp 487–504, esp pp. 492–5.
51. Russell, *The First Modern Arab State*, pp 179–80.
52. Doc 284, *DBFP First Series Vol. XIII.*

7 Reversals of Fortune 1920–5

1. For background on Ibn Saud see Yapp, *The Making of the Modern Near East*, p 60.
2. Teitelbaum, *The Rise and Fall of the Hashemite Kingdom of Arabia*, p 103.
3. This section leans heavily on J Kostiner, 'Prologue of Hashemite Downfall and Saudi Ascendancy: A New Look at the Khurma dispute', in A Susser and A Shmuelevitz (eds), *The Hashemites in the Modern Arab World: Essays in Honour of the Late Professor Uriel Dann* (Frank Cass, London: 1995) pp 47–65.
4. Mary C Wilson, *King Abdullah, Britain, and the Making of Jordan*. Cambridge Middle East Library (Cambridge University Press, Cambridge: 1987) p 37.
5. War Office 32/5619, Paper on proposed kingdom of Mesopotamia and the advantages and disadvantages of making Emir Faisal first King.
6. Busch, *Britain, India, and the Arabs, 1914–1921*, p 333.
7. Teitelbaum, *The Rise and Fall of the Hashemite Kingdom of Arabia*, p 198.

8. Teitelbaum, *The Rise and Fall of the Hashimite Kingdom of Arabia*, p 166.
9. Wilson, *Lawrence of Arabia*, p 656.
10. Wilson, *Lawrence of Arabia*, pp 656, 657–61.
11. Wilson, *King Abdullah, Britain, and the Making of Jordan*, pp 41–3.
12. Kamal S Salibi, *The Modern History of Jordan* (I.B. Tauris, London: 1993) p 83.
13. See Wilson, *King Abdullah, Britain, and the Making of Jordan*, Chapter 4.
14. TNA FO 608/97–0008, Future government of Mesopotamia: Memorandum by Emir Faisal 23 Jun 1919.
15. TNA FO 608/97–0016, Curzon to Clayton 24 Jun 1919.
16. G Bell to her Mother, 12 Jan 1920.
17. G Bell to her Mother, 14 Mar 1920.
18. G Bell to her Mother, 10 Apr 1920.
19. D K Fieldhouse, *Western Imperialism in the Middle East 1914–1958* (Oxford University Press, Oxford: 2006) p 86.
20. Busch, *Britain, India, and the Arabs, 1914–1921*, p 408.
21. Wilson, *Lawrence of Arabia*, pp 639–40.
22. *Churchill Companion IV, 1917–1922*, Pt II, p 829.
23. *Churchill Companion IV, 1917–1922*, Pt II, pp 937–9.
24. Darwin, *Britain, Egypt and the Middle East*, pp 39–40.
25. *Churchill Companion IV, 1917–1922*, Pt II, p 1279.
26. Paris, 'British Middle East Policy-Making after the First World War', pp 773–93.
27. Darwin, *Britain, Egypt and the Middle East*, p 216.
28. *Churchill Companion IV, 1917–1922*, Pt II, pp 1300, 1303–6.
29. Monroe, *Britain's Moment in the Middle East*, pp 35–6.
30. Wilson, *Lawrence of Arabia*, pp 641–2.

31. Karsh and Karsh, *Empires of the Sand*, p 308.
32. Wilson, *Lawrence of Arabia*, p 643.
33. *Churchill Companion IV, 1917–1922*, Pt II, p 1334.
34. The best account remains Aaron S Klieman, *Foundations of British Policy in the Arab World: The Cairo Conference of 1921* (Johns Hopkins Press, Baltimore: 1970).
35. Sachar, *The Emergence of the Middle East*, p 378.
36. Sachar, *The Emergence of the Middle East*, pp 402–3; Wilson, *Lawrence of Arabia*, p 649; Fromkin, *A Peace to End All Peace*, p 504.
37. Wilson, *King Abdullah, Britain, and the Making of Jordan*, pp 52–3.
38. Klieman, *Foundations of British Policy in the Arab World*, p 124.
39. Wilson, *Lawrence of Arabia*, p 650.
40. *Churchill Companion IV, 1917–1922*, Pt III, pp 1553–4.
41. Phebe Marr, *The Modern History of Iraq* (Westview Press, Boulder, Colo: 2004) p 25.
42. Darwin, *Britain, Egypt and the Middle East*, p 37.
43. *Churchill Companion IV, 1917–1922*, Pt III, p 1675.
44. *Churchill Companion IV, 1917–1922*, Pt III, pp 1974–7.
45. Wilson, *Lawrence of Arabia*, p 662.
46. Kamal S Salibi, *The Modern History of Jordan* (I.B. Tauris, London: 1993) p 88.
47. Avi Shlaim, *Lion of Jordan: The Life of King Hussein in War and Peace* (Allen Lane, London: 2007) p 17.

8 The Peace Treaties and the Fate of the Arab Lands

1. The history of Iraq since independence is well served by the seminal Hanna Batatu's *Old Social Classes and the Revolutionary Movements of Iraq: A Study of*

Iraq's Old Landed and Commercial Classes and of Its Communists, Ba'thists, and Free Officers (Princeton, London: 1978). Two excellent general accounts are the aforementioned Marr, *The Modern History of Iraq*, and Charles Tripp, *A History of Iraq* (Cambridge University Press, Cambridge: 2001).

2. Marr, *The Modern History of Iraq*, p 30.
3. William Roger Louis, *Ends of British Imperialism: the Scramble for Empire, Suez and Decolonization: Collected Essays* (I.B. Tauris, London: 2006) p 862.
4. See Peter Sluggett, *Britain in Iraq: Contriving King and Country* 2nd ed (I.B. Tauris, London: 2007) pp 108–20.
5. Marr, *The Modern History of Iraq*, p 34.
6. Tripp, *A History of Iraq*, pp 61–2.
7. Cited in Khaldun S Husry, 'King Faysal I and Arab Unity, 1930–33', *Journal of Contemporary History* 10:2 (1975) p 324.
8. Sluggett, *Britain in Iraq*, p 94; Tripp, *A History of Iraq*, pp 61–2.
9. Marr, *The Modern History of Iraq*, pp 44–6.
10. For the 1941 coup and its aftermath see Marr, *The Modern History of Iraq*, pp 53–6; and Tripp, *A History of Iraq*, pp 99–106.
11. See Wilson, *King Abdullah, Britain and the Making of Jordan*, pp 129–68.
12. Avi Shlaim, *Collusion across the Jordan: King Abdullah, the Zionist Movement and the Partition of Palestine* (Clarendon Press, Oxford: 1988).
13. Avi Shlaim, *The Iron Wall: Israel and the Arab World* (Penguin, London: 2001) pp 62–8.
14. Shlaim, *Lion of Jordan: The Life of King Hussein in War and Peace* is a sympathetic account of his life.

15. Tripp, *A History of Iraq*, pp 125–6.
16. See Robert McNamara, *Britain, Nasser and the Balance of Power in the Middle East* (Cass, Portland: 2003) pp 42–6.
17. Louis, *Ends of British Imperialism*, p 860.
18. Stephen Longrigg and Frank Stoakes, *Iraq* (Praeger, New York: 1959) p 225.
19. See George Lawrence Harris, *Iraq: Its People, Its Society, Its Culture* (HRAF Press, New Haven: 1958) p 83; Longrigg and Stoakes, *Iraq*, p 242.
20. Sluggett, *Britain in Iraq*, p 213.
21. On the revolt and its wider international repercussions see Joyce Laverty Miller, 'The Syrian Revolt of 1925', *International Journal of Middle East Studies*, Vol 8, No 4 (Oct 1977), pp 545–63; and Martin Thomas, 'The Syrian Revolt and Anglo-French imperial relations, 1925–27', in G C Kennedy and K Neilson (eds), *Incidents and International Relations: People, Power, and Personalities* (Praeger, Westport, Conn: 2002) pp 65–86.
22. Phillip S Khoury, *Syria and the French Mandate: The Politics of Arab Nationalism, 1920–1945* (Princeton University Press, Princeton, N.J.:1987) p 205.
23. Laverty Miller, 'The Syrian Revolt of 1925', p 547.
24. Miller, 'The Syrian Revolt of 1925', pp 545–6.
25. Malcolm E Yapp, *The Near East Since the First World War: A History to 1995*. A History of the Near East (Longman, Harlow: 2007) pp 96–7.
26. The best guide to the intra-Arab battle for Syria remains Patrick Seale, *The Struggle for Syria: A Study of Post-War Arab Politics, 1945–1958* (Oxford University Press, Oxford 1965).

27. For Assad's career and the Lebanon see Patrick Seale and Maureen McConville, *Assad of Syria: The Struggle for the Middle East* (University of California Press, Berkeley: 1989).

Conclusion

1. Yapp, *The Near East since the First World War*, p 3.
2. A Drysdale and G Blake, *The Middle East and North Africa: A Political Geography* (Oxford University Press, Oxford: 1985) p2 25 cited in Ian S *Lustick* (1997), 'The Absence of Middle Eastern Great Powers: Political "Backwardness" in Historical Perspective', *International Organization* 51:4 (Autumn 1997) pp 653–83.

Chronology

YEAR	THE LIVES AND THE LAND
1853	Birth of Hussein ibn Ali in Constantinople. 4 Oct: Ottoman Sultan declares war on Russia in opening stage of Crimean War.
1891	Hussein ibn Ali resides in Constantinople as forced guest of the Sultan until 1908.
1908	Completion of Hejaz railway. Jun–Jul: Young Turk Revolution and restoration of Ottoman constitution. Nov: Return of Hussein to Mecca as Grand Sherif and Emir.
1914	Feb & Sep: Abdullah's initial contacts with British in Cairo. Nov: Turkey at war with Entente Powers. Britain gives pledge of Arab independence.
1915	Mar: Dardenelles Campaign (to Jan 1916). Damascus Protocol is given to Feisal by Syrian nationalists. Jul: Correspondence between Hussein and Sir Henry McMahon (to Feb 1916).

YEAR	HISTORY	CULTURE
1853	Haussman begins reconstruction of Paris. First railway through the Alps completed.	Charlotte Brontë, *Villette*. Verdi, *La Traviata*.
1891	Franco-Russian entente. Young Turk Movement founded in Vienna.	Tchaikovsky, *The Nutcracker Suite*.
1908	*The Daily Telegraph* publishes remarks about German hostility towards England made by Kaiser Wilhelm II. Ferdinand I declares Bulgaria's independence and assumes the title of Tsar.	Colette, *La Retraite Sentimentale*. E M Forster, *A Room with a View*. For the first time, Matisse calls a painting by Braque 'Cubist'.
1914	Archduke Franz Ferdinand of Austria-Hungary and his wife are assassinated in Sarajevo. Outbreak of First World War: Battles of Mons, the Marne and First Ypres: trench warfare on the Western Front.	James Joyce, *Dubliners*. Marcel Duchamp exhibits *Readymades* in Paris. Film: Charlie Chaplin in *Making a Living*.
1915	First World War: Battles of Neuve Chappelle and Loos. The 'Shells Scandal'. Germans sink the British liner *Lusitania,* killing 1,198.	John Buchan, *The Thirty-Nine Steps*. Ezra Pound, *Cathay*. Film: *The Birth of a Nation*.

YEAR	THE LIVES AND THE LAND
1916	Apr: Surrender of British force at Kut in Mesopotamia.
	May: Sykes-Picot Agreement finalised.
	Jul: Outbreak of Arab Revolt.
	Oct: Beginning of T E Lawrence's involvement with Arab Revolt.
1917	Jan: Capture of Wajh by Arab irregulars.
	Jul: Capture of Akaba by Arab irregulars.
	Nov: Balfour Declaration promises homeland in Palestine for Jews.
	Nov: Sykes-Picot agreement is revealed by Bolsheviks.
	Dec: Capture of Jerusalem by British Imperial forces.
1918	Jun: Declaration to the Seven by Britain and France promising Arab independence.
	Sep: Capture of Damascus by British and Arab forces.
	Oct: Armistice of Mudros ends war with Turkey.
	Nov: Anglo-French Declaration affirming commitments to Arabs.

YEAR	HISTORY	CULTURE
1916	First World War. Western Front: Battle of Verdun, Battle of the Somme. US President Woodrow Wilson is re-elected. Lloyd George becomes Prime Minister.	Vicente Blasco Ibanez, *The Four Horsemen of the Apocalypse*. Film: *Intolerance*.
1917	First World War. February Revolution in Russia. USA declares war on Germany. China declares war on Germany and Russia. German and Russian delegates sign armistice at Brest-Litovsk.	P G Wodehouse, *The Man With Two Left Feet*. Prokofiev, 'Classical Symphony'. Film: *Easy Street*.
1918	First World War. Peace Treaty of Brest-Litovsk between Russia and the Central Powers. German Spring offensives on Western Front fail. Successful Allied offensives on Western Front. Armistice signed between Allies and Germany; German Fleet surrenders; Kaiser Wilhelm II abdicates.	Luigi Pirandello, *Six Characters in Search of an Author*. Edvard Munch, *Bathing Man*.

YEAR	THE LIVES AND THE LAND
1919	Jan: Paris Peace Conference affirms that Arab provinces will not be restored to Ottoman rule.
	Feisal/Chaim Weizmann agreement accepts Jewish immigration into Palestine but conditional on Arab independence in Syria.
	Feb: Feisal addresses Peace Conference.
	May: Defeat of Abdullah at Khurma by *Ikhwan* warriors of Ibn Saud.
	Jun–Aug: King-Crane Commission visits Middle East and recommends against a French Mandate.
	Sep: British withdrawal from Syria.
1920	Jan: Feisal-Clemenceau agreement.
	Mar: Declaration of Independence by Syrian National Congress and proclamation of Feisal as King.
	Apr: San Remo Conference on Mandates rejects independence for Syria.
	Jun: Widespread disorder in Mesopotamia in protest against British rule (to Dec).
	Jul–Aug: French military action in Syria sees expulsion of Feisal and supporters and French rule established.
	Aug: Treaty of Sèvres signed by Mehmet VI, accepting the Allies' terms demanding huge territorial concessions by Turkey including the Arab lands.
1921	Jan: Winston Churchill made British Colonial Secretary and tasked with resolving Middle East unrest.
	Mar: Cairo conference of Middle East experts convened by Churchill. It recommends the Crown of Iraq is offered and that Feisal and Transjordan be separated from Palestine.
	Apr: Abdullah made ruler of Tranjordan for six-month period.
	23 Aug: Feisal crowned King of Iraq.

YEAR	HISTORY	CULTURE
1919	Communist Revolt in Berlin. Benito Mussolini founds fascist movement in Italy. British-Persian agreement at Tehran to preserve integrity of Persia. Irish War of Independence begins. US Senate votes against ratification of Versailles Treaty, leaving the USA outside the League of Nations.	Bauhaus movement founded by Walter Gropius. Thomas Hardy, *Collected Poems.* George Bernard Shaw, *Heartbreak House.* Film: *The Cabinet of Dr Caligari.*
1920	League of Nations comes into existence. The Hague is selected as seat of International Court of Justice. League of Nations headquarters moved to Geneva. Bolsheviks win Russian Civil War. Adolf Hitler announces his 25-point programme in Munich.	F Scott Fitzgerald, *This Side of Paradise.* Franz Kafka, *The Country Doctor.* Katherine Mansfield, *Bliss.* Rambert School of Ballet formed.
1921	Irish Free State established. Peace treaty signed between Russia and Germany. State of Emergency proclaimed in Germany in the face of economic crisis. Washington Naval Treaty signed.	Aldous Huxley, *Chrome Yellow.* D H Lawrence, *Women in Love.* John Dos Passos, *Three Soldiers.* Salzburg Festival established.

YEAR	THE LIVES AND THE LAND
1922	Jul: League of Nations formally ratifies Mandate system: Iraq, Palestine and Transjordan to Britain, rest to France. Oct: Anglo-Iraqi treaty reluctantly agreed by Feisal.
1923	May: Britain recognises Transjordan as Mandate being guided to independence, with Abdullah confirmed as ruler under British supervision. Jul: Treaty of Lausanne supersedes Treaty of Sèvres with Turkey.
1924	Mar: Turkish National Assembly abolishes caliphate. Hussein claims title of Caliph. Sep–Oct: Invasion of Hejaz; capture of Mecca and Taif by Ibn Saud and the *Ihkwan*. Oct: Flight of Hussein to Cyprus.
1925	Oct: Druze revolt in Syria sees fighting in Damascus. Dec: Fall of Medina and end of Kingdom of Hejaz (to Jan 1926).
1930	Nov: Anglo-Iraqi Treaty.
1931	Jun: Death of Hussein in Amman.
1932	Oct: Iraq admitted to League of Nations – end of Mandate.
1933	Kingdom of Saudi Arabia established. Oct: Death of Feisal I of Iraq; succession of his son, Ghazi.

YEAR	HISTORY	CULTURE
1922	Chanak Crisis. Britain recognises Kingdom of Egypt under Fuad I.	F Scott Fitzgerald, *The Beautiful and Damned.* British Broadcasting Company (later Corporation) (BBC) founded: first radio broadcasts.
1923	French and Belgian troops occupy the Ruhr when Germany fails to make reparation payments. The USSR formally comes into existence. Adolf Hitler's *coup d'état* (The Beer Hall Putsch) fails.	Edna St Vincent Millay, *The Ballad of the Harp-Weaver; A Few Figs from Thistles.* Kandinsky, *Circle within Circle.* George Gershwin, 'Rhapsody in Blue'.
1924	Death of Lenin. Dawes Plan published. Greece is proclaimed a republic. Labour Party loses general election after *Daily Mail* publishes the Zinoviev Letter.	Noel Coward, *The Vortex.* E M Forster, *A Passage to India.* Puccini, *Turandot.* Picasso, *Great Harlequin.*
1925	In Italy, Mussolini announces that he will take dictatorial powers. Pound Sterling returns to the Gold Standard.	Virginia Woolf, *Mrs Dalloway.* Georges Balachine choreographer of the *Ballets Russes* in Paris. Film: *Battleship Potemkin.*
1930	London Naval Treaty signed.	Noel Coward, *Private Lives.*
1931	National Government formed in Great Britain.	Films: *Dracula. Little Caesar.*
1932	F D Roosevelt wins US Presidential election.	Aldous Huxley, *Brave New World.*
1933	Adolf Hitler is appointed Chancellor of Germany. Japan and Germany leave the League of Nations.	George Orwell, *Down and Out in Paris and London.* Film: *King Kong.*

YEAR	THE LIVES AND THE LAND
1936	Oct: First of series of military coups in Iraq usher in era of dominance by military until 1941.
1939	Apr: Ghazi I dies in a car accident and his son Feisal II is installed at age of four. Regency of Ghazi's cousin, Prince Abdullah.
1941	Apr–May: British invasion and 'second occupation' of Iraq as a result of pro-Axis nationalists taking power. Jun: British invasion and occupation of French-ruled Syria.
1945	Creation of the Arab League.
1946	Mar: End of Mandate in Transjordan. Abdullah becomes King of renamed Kingdom of Jordan. Apr: French forces evacuate Syria and Lebanon.
1948	Arab-Israeli War; Abdullah's forces occupy West Bank and East Jerusalem.
1951	Jul: Assassination of Abdullah; he is succeeded by his son Talal who suffers from a debilitating mental illness.
1953	Hussein becomes King of Jordan upon abdication of Talal.
1955	Feb–Apr: Nuri al Said, Prime Minister of Iraq, takes lead in formation of Baghdad Pact.
1956	Oct–Nov: Suez Crisis: major factor in increase in popularity of President Nasser of Egypt and his radical pan-Arab agenda.

YEAR	HISTORY	CULTURE
1936	German troops occupy Rhineland. Outbreak of Spanish Civil War.	Berlin Olympics. Films: *Modern Times. Camille.*
1939	German invasion of Poland: Britain and France declare war. Soviets invade Finland.	John Steinbeck, *The Grapes of Wrath.* Film: *The Wizard of Oz.*
1941	Second World War. Germany invades USSR. Japan attacks Pearl Harbor. Germany and Italy declare war on the USA.	Bertold Brecht, *Mother Courage and Her Children.* Film: *Citizen Kane.*
1945	End of the Second World War.	Evelyn Waugh, *Brideshead Revisited.*
1946	Churchill declares that Stalin has lowered an 'Iron Curtain', signalling the formal start of the Cold War. Nuremberg establishes guilty verdicts for war crimes.	Bertrand Russell, *History of Western Philosophy.* Films: *Great Expectations. It's a Wonderful Life.*
1948	Gandhi is assassinated in India: last British troops leave India. Berlin Airlift.	Graham Greene, *The Heart of the Matter.* Film: *Whisky Galore.*
1951	Korean War: Chinese forces take Seoul.	Isaac Asimov, *Foundation.* Film: *A Streetcar Named Desire.*
1953	Death of Stalin. Armistice signed in Korea.	Arthur Miller, *The Crucible.* Film: *Gentlemen Prefer Blondes.*
1955	Churchill resigns as Prime Minister: replaced by Anthony Eden.	Graham Greene, *The Quiet American.*

YEAR	THE LIVES AND THE LAND
1957	Apr: Governmental crisis in Jordan.
	Aug–Nov: Crisis in Syria caused by intra-Arab infighting and Cold War intrigue.
1958	Feb: Formation of United Arab Republic by Egypt and Syria; formation of Arab Union by Jordan and Iraq.
	Jul: Revolution in Iraq ends Hashemite monarchy.
1994	Oct: Israeli-Jordanian Peace Treaty ends state of war after 46 years.

YEAR	HISTORY	CULTURE
1957	Belgium, France, West Germany, Italy, Luxembourg and Netherlands sign Treaty of Rome establishing the European Economic Community (EEC).	Jack Kerouac, *On the Road*. Film: *The Bridge on the River Kwai*.
1958	Charles de Gaulle elected president of French Republic.	Boris Pasternak, *Dr Zhivago*. Film: *Vertigo*.
1994	Nelson Mandela is sworn in as president of South Africa.	Films: *The Madness of King George*. *Pulp Fiction*.

Bibliographical Note

The subject of the First World War, the Peace Settlement and its aftermath in the Middle East has generated a vast bibliography of popular and academic studies. This note only refers to those I found most useful in preparing this book. The Hashemites have also received considerable scholarly attention. Margaret MacMillan's *Peacemakers* provides an excellent introduction to the subject of the Middle East at the Peace Conference. Broad overviews of Middle Eastern history include the late Albert Hourani's justly acclaimed *A History of the Arab Peoples.* (2005 edition) and Ira Lapidus's massive study *A History of Islamic Societies* (2002 edition). Both are focused more on developments within the region and its societies than the influence of external powers. Lapidus' work, as its title indicates, has a broader compass that ranges beyond the Middle East. Both are highly sophisticated works of history and broadly sympathetic to the region and its inhabitants. Peter Mansfield, *A History of the Middle East* (2004) is much more focused on the international history of the region and the impact of foreign powers.

The best general account of the Middle East in the period from the French Revolution to the First World War is Malcolm

Yapp's excellent *The Making of the Modern Near East,
1792–1923* (1987). Two useful books that cover the period
from 1914 to 1922 in great detail are Howard Morley Sachar,
The Emergence of the Middle East, 1914–1924 (1970) and
the more recent and best-selling David Fromkin, *A Peace to
End All Peace: Creating the Modern Middle East, 1914–1922*
(1989). Both view the Middle East very much from a Euro-
centric point of view and are primarily based on the excellent
collections of British documents produced under the *Documents on British Foreign Policy 1919–1939* series. Fromkin's
volume has the advantage of building on the vast documentation in the relevant companion volumes of Martin Gilbert's
official biography of Winston Churchill. Both Fromkin and
Sachar are clearly influenced by the late Elie Kedourie, who
wrote two of the key texts on Britain's relations with the
Hashemites in *England and the Middle East* (1956) and *In the
Anglo-Arab Labyrinth: The McMahon-Husayn Correspondence and Its Interpretations, 1914–1939* (1976). Kedourie was
a tireless interpreter of the vast documentation on the First
World War Middle East in the British National Archives. He
tends to be a harsh critic of the Hashemites and those British
politicians and administrators who accepted their version of
British betrayal as articulated in George Antonius' *The Arab
Awakening* (1939). Isaiah Friedman's *The Question of Palestine, 1914–1918: British-Jewish-Arab Relations* (1973) is
another book sceptical of the Hashemite viewpoint. Both
Kedourie and Friedman are challenged by Charles D Smith
in his article 'The Invention of a Tradition: The Question
of Arab Acceptance of the Zionist Right to Palestine during
World War I' in the *Journal of Palestine Studies* (Winter
1993). More recently Efraim and Inari Karsh have followed
on from the Kedourie position and extended it into an even

harsher critique of the Hashemites, Arab nationalism and Islamic imperialism in a series of books and articles, most notably in *Empires of the Sand: The Struggle for Mastery in the Middle East, 1789–1923* (1999). The Karshs' work is characterised by wide-ranging research, judgemental conclusions and a very hostile tone towards the Hashemites.

The Hashemites have been the subject of a number of studies. The dearth of primary source material means they tend to be based on British, and to a lesser extent, French documents. The only memoir is Abdullah's *Memoirs of King Abdullah of Transjordan* (1950). J. Nevo assesses its value in his essay 'Abdullah's memoirs as historical source material' in Asher Susser and Aryeh Shmuelevitz (eds), *The Hashemites in the Modern Arab World: Essays in Honour of the Late Professor Uriel Dann* (1995). Mary C Wilson, *King Abdullah, Britain, and the Making of Jordan* (1987) is a study of his relations with Britain but contains a wealth of biographical material. Feisal, perhaps the most interesting Hashemite, is given voice in Beatrice Erskine, *King Faisal of Iraq: An Authorised and Authentic Study* (1933), which was based partly on interviews with him before his premature death. A popular and highly readable biographical study of the family is James Morris, *The Hashemite Kings* (1959). Hussein has received coverage ranging from the hagiographic in Randall Baker, *King Husain and the Kingdom of Hejaz* (1979) to the insightful and critical work of Joshua Teitelbaum in a number of books and articles, most notably *The Rise and Fall of the Hashimite Kingdom of Arabia* (2001).

Arab nationalism is central to this story. Approaches include the classic interpretation of Antonius which viewed Arab nationalism as an organic vibrant force even before the First World War. C Ernest Dawn, whose work beginning more than 40 years ago is perhaps best encapsulated in *From Ottomanism to Arabism; Essays on the Origins of Arab Nationalism* (1973) frames much of the current debate. There are important syntheses in the essays in Rashid Khalidi *et al*, *The Origins of Arab Nationalism* (1991) and in A Dawisha, *Arab Nationalism in the Twentieth Century: From Triumph to Despair* (2003). Eliezer Tauber, *The Emergence of the Arab Movements* (1993) and *The Formation of Modern Syria and Iraq* (1995) are recent detailed reconstructions of Arab national movements before, during and after the War based on huge research. A useful counterpoint is the critical essay on Arab nationalism by Efraim and Inari Karsh, 'Myth in the desert, or not the Great Arab Revolt' in the journal *Middle Eastern Studies* (1997).

British policy during the war and its aftermath is well covered in Jukka Nevakivi, *Britain, France and the Arab Middle East 1914–1920* and Timothy J Paris, *Britain, the Hashemites, and Arab Rule, 1920–1925: The Sherifian Solution* (2003) as well as Fromkin and Sachar. The best overview contextualising half a century of British Middle Eastern policy remains Elizabeth Monroe's acclaimed classic *Britain's Moment in the Middle East 1914–1956* (1963). D K Fieldhouse, *Western Imperialism in the Middle East 1914–1958* (2006), is an excellent modern assessment. French policy can be traced in Jan Karl Tanenbaum's lengthy essay 'France and the Arab Middle East, 1914–1920' in *Transactions of the American Philosophical Society* (1978) and C M Andrew and A S Kanya-Forstner, *France Overseas: The Great War and the Climax of French Imperial Expansion* (1981).

The fall of Feisal's kingdom in Syria is the subject of Zeine N Zeine, *The Struggle for Arab Independence; Western Diplomacy & the Rise and Fall of Faisal's Kingdom in Syria*

(1960), Malcolm Russell, *The First Modern Arab State: Syria Under Faysal, 1918–1920* (1985) and James Gelvin's *Divided Loyalties: Nationalism and Mass Politics in Syria at the Close of Empire* (1998). The fate of the successor states, Syria, Iraq and Jordan, can be traced in Charles Tripp, *A History of Iraq* (2002), P Marr, *The Modern History of Iraq* (2004 edition), Kamal S Salibi, *The Modern History of Jordan* and Philip S Khoury, *Syria and the French Mandate: The Politics of Arab Nationalism, 1920–1945* (1987). The post-First World War history of the entire Middle East is skilfully drawn in Malcolm Yapp, *The Near East Since the First World War: A History to 1995* (1996).

A wealth of articles can be found in the following journals: *The Historical Journal, International Journal of Middle East Studies, Journal of Palestine Studies* and *Middle Eastern Studies*. The middle two tend to reflect a line sympathetic to the Arab cause, while *Middle Eastern Studies* was founded and edited for many years by Elie Kedourie and reflects his sceptical line.

Bibliography

Documentary Collections

Bury, J P T, and Rohan Butler, *Documents on British Foreign Policy: 1919 – 1939* Series 1, Vol 13 (H.M.S.O., London: 1963).

Commission de publication des documents diplomatiques français, *Documents diplomatiques français.* 1920 (Imprimerie nationale, Paris: 2003).

Gilbert, Martin, *Winston S. Churchill/Companion* Volume 4, Pt 1, 2, 3 (Houghton Mifflin Company, Boston MA: 1978).

Hurewitz, Jacob C, *The Middle East and North Africa in World Politics* 2 (Yale University Press, New Haven: 1979).

Mantoux, Paul, Arthur Stanley Link, and Manfred F Boemeke, *The Deliberations of the Council of Four (March 24-June 28, 1919).* Supplementary volumes to the papers of Woodrow Wilson (Princeton University Press, Princeton, N.J.: 1992).

Papers Relating to the Foreign Relations of the United States, 1919: The Paris Peace Conference, 13 volumes (US Government Printing Office, Washington, D.C.: 1942–7).

Wilson, Woodrow, and Arthur Stanley Link, *The Papers of Woodrow Wilson*, Vols 55–66 (Princeton University Press, Princeton, N.J.: 1986–92).

Woodward, E L, and Rohan Butler, *Documents on British Foreign Policy 1919–1939*. Series 1, Vol 4 (H.M.S.O, London: 1952).

Reference

Ovendale, Ritchie, *The Longman Companion to the Middle East Since 1914* (Addison Wesley Longman, New York: 1998).

Sela, Avraham, *The Continuum Political Encyclopedia of the Middle East* (Continuum, New York: 2002).

Websites

Gertrude Bell's Letters and Diaries at http://www.gerty.ncl.ac.uk/

T E Lawrence's biographer Jeremy Wilson has assembled a superb collection of out-of-copyright documents, including Arab Bureau material, letters and writings at the T E Lawrence Studies website http://www.telstudies.org/

List of works cited

Abdullah, *Memoirs of King Abdullah of Transjordan* (Cape, London: 1950).

Alangari, Haifa, *The Struggle for Power in Arabia: Ibn Saud, Hussein and Great Britain, 1914–1924* (Ithaca Press, Reading: 1998).

Aldington, Richard, *Lawrence of Arabia: A Biographical Enquiry* (Collins, London: 1955).

Anderson, M S, *The Eastern Question, 1774–1923: A Study in International Relations* (Macmillan, London: 1966).

Andrew, Christopher M, and A S Kanya-Forstner, *France Overseas: The Great War and the Climax of French Imperial Expansion* (Thames and Hudson, London: 1981).

Antonius, George, *The Arab Awakening: The Story of the Arab National Movement* (Putnam, New York: 1946).

Baker, Randall, *King Husain and the Kingdom of Hejaz* (Oleander Press, Cambridge: 1979).

Barr, James, *Setting the Desert on Fire: T.E. Lawrence and Britain's Secret War in Arabia, 1916–18* (Bloomsbury, London: 2006).

Batatu, Hanna, *The Old Social Classes and the Revolutionary Movements of Iraq: A Study of Iraq's Old Landed and Commercial Classes and of Its Communists, Bathists, and Free Officers.* Princeton studies on the Near East (Princeton University Press, Princeton, N.J.: 1978).

Bonsal, Stephen, *Suitors and Suppliants: The Little Nations at Versailles* (Prentice-Hall, inc, New York: 1946).

Boyle, S S, *Betrayal in Palestine: the story of George Antonius* (Westview Press, Boulder, Colo: 2001).

Busch, Briton Cooper, *Britain, India, and the Arabs, 1914–1921* (University of California Press, Berkeley: 1971).

Buzpinar, Tufan, 'Opposition to the Ottoman Caliphate in the Early Years of Abdülhamid II: 1877–1882', *Die Welt des Islams*, New Ser Vol 36, Issue 1 (Mar 1996) pp 59–89.

Darwin, John, *Britain, Egypt and the Middle East: Imperial Policy in the Aftermath of War 1918–1922.* Cambridge Commonwealth series (Macmillan, London: 1981).

Dawisha, A I, *Arab Nationalism in the Twentieth Century: From Triumph to Despair* (Princeton University Press, Princeton, N.J.: 2003).

Dawn, C Ernest, 'The Amir of Mecca Al-Husayn Ibn-'Ali and the Origin of the Arab Revolt' *Proceedings of the American Philosophical Society*, Vol 104, No 1 (15 Feb 1960) pp 11–34.

——, 'From Ottomanism to Arabism: The Origin of an Ideology', *The Review of Politics*, Vol 23, No 3 (Jul 1961) pp 378–400.

——, *From Ottomanism to Arabism; Essays on the Origins of Arab Nationalism* (University of Illinois Press, Urbana: 1973).

——, 'The Origins of Arab Nationalism', in Rashid Khalidi *et al* (eds), *The Origins of Arab Nationalism* (Columbia University Press, New York: 1991).

Dann, Uriel, *Iraq Under Qassem; A Political History, 1958–1963* (Praeger, New York: 1969).

——, *The Great Powers in the Middle East, 1919–1939* (Holmes & Meier, New York: 1988).

Erskine, Beatrice, *King Faisal of Iraq: An Authorised and Authentic Study* (Hutchinson, London: 1933).

Farouk-Sluglett, Marion, and Peter Sluglett, *Iraq Since 1958: From Revolution to Dictatorship* (KPI, London: 1987).

Fieldhouse, D K, *Western Imperialism in the Middle East 1914–1958* (Oxford University Press, Oxford: 2006).

Fisher, John, 'Syria and Mesopotamia in British Middle Eastern Policy in 1919', *Middle Eastern Studies* 34:2 (Apr 1998) pp 129–70.

——, *Curzon and British Imperialism in the Middle East, 1916–19* (Frank Cass, London: 1999).

Fitzgerald, Edward Peter, 'France's Middle Eastern Ambitions, the Sykes-Picot Negotiations, and the Oil Fields of Mosul, 1915–1918', *The Journal of Modern History*, Vol 66, No 4 (Dec 1994) pp 697–725.

Friedman, Isaiah, *The Question of Palestine, 1914–1918; British-Jewish-Arab Relations* (Schocken Books, New York: 1973).

Fromkin, David. *A Peace to End All Peace: Creating the Modern Middle East, 1914–1922* (Deutsch, London: 1989).

Garnett, David (ed), *The Letters of T. E. Lawrence* (Jonathan Cape, London: 1938).

Gelvin, James L, 'The Ironic Legacy of the King-Crane Commission' in Lesch, David W, *The Middle East and the United States: A Historical and Political Reassessment* (Westview Press, Boulder, Colo: 1996).

——, *Divided Loyalties: Nationalism and Mass Politics in Syria at the Close of Empire* (University of California Press, Berkeley: 1998).

Gilbert, Martin, *World in Torment: Winston S. Churchill, 1916–1922* (Minerva, London: 1990).

Gooch, G P, and Harold William Vazeille Temperley, *British Documents on the Origins of the War, 1898–1914*, Vol X, Part II (H.M.S.O., London: 1938).

Haim, Sylvia G, '"The Arab Awakening", A Source for the Historian?' *Die Welt des Islams,* II (1953).

Harris, George Lawrence, *Iraq: Its People, Its Society, Its Culture* (HRAF Press, New Haven: 1958).

Headlam, James Wycliffe, Agnes Headlam-Morley, Russell Bryant and Anna M Cienciala, *A Memoir of the Paris Peace Conference, 1919* (Methuen, London: 1972).

Hinnebusch, Raymond A, *Authoritarian Power and State Formation in Ba'thist Syria: Army, Party, and Peasant.* Westview Special Studies on the Middle East (Westview Press, Boulder, Colo: 1990).

Hopwood, Derek (ed), *Studies in Arab History: the Antonius lectures, 1978–87* (Macmillan, Basingstoke: 1990).

Hourani, Albert Habib, '"*The Arab Awakening*" Forty Years Later', in Derek Hopwood (ed), *Studies in Arab History: The Antonius Lectures, 1978–87* (Macmillan, Basingstoke: 1990).

——, *A History of the Arab Peoples* (Faber, London: 2005).

Howard, Harry N, *The King-Crane Commission: An American Inquiry in the Middle East* (Khayats, Beirut: 1963).

Hurewitz, Jacob C, *The Middle East and North Africa in World Politics* 2 (Yale University Press, New Haven: 1979).

Husry, Khaldun S, 'King Faysal I and Arab Unity, 1930–33', *Journal of Contemporary History* 10:2 (1975) pp 323–40.

James, Lawrence, *The Golden Warrior: The Life and Legend of Lawrence of Arabia* (Abacus, London: 1996).

Karsh, Efraim, and Inari Karsh, 'Myth in the desert, or not the Great Arab Revolt', *Middle Eastern Studies* 33:2 (1997) pp 267–312.

——, *Empires of the Sand: The Struggle for Mastery in the Middle East, 1789–1923* (Harvard University Press, Cambridge, MA: 1999).

Kedourie, Elie, *England and the Middle East* (Bowes & Bowes, London: 1956).

———, *In the Anglo-Arab Labyrinth: The McMahon-Husayn Correspondence and Its Interpretations, 1914–1939* (Cambridge University Press, Cambridge: 1976).

Kennedy, Greg, and Keith Neilson, *Incidents and International Relations: People, Power, and Personalities* (Praeger, Westport, Conn: 2002).

Kent, Marian, *Oil and Empire: British Policy and Mesopotamian Oil 1900–1920* (Macmillan, London: 1976).

——— (ed), *The Great Powers and the End of the Ottoman Empire* (G. Allen & Unwin, London: 1984).

———, 'Great Britain and the End of the Ottoman Empire, 1900–23' in Marian Kent (ed), *The Great Powers and the End of the Ottoman Empire* (G. Allen & Unwin, London: 1984).

Khadduri, Majid, *Republican Iraq; A Study in Iraqi Politics Since the Revolution of 1958* (Oxford University Press, London: 1969).

———, *Political Trends in the Arab World: The Role of Ideas and Ideals in Politics* (John Hopkins Press, Baltimore: 1970)

Khalidi, Rashid, *et al* (eds), *The Origins of Arab Nationalism* (Columbia University Press, New York: 1991).

Khoury, Philip S, *Syria and the French Mandate: The Politics of Arab Nationalism, 1920–1945*. Princeton Studies on the Near East (Princeton University Press, Princeton, N.J.: 1987).

Klieman, Aaron S, *Foundations of British Policy in the Arab World: The Cairo Conference of 1921* (Johns Hopkins Press, Baltimore: 1970).

Kramer, Martin S, *Arab Awakening and Islamic Revival: The Politics of Ideas in the Middle East* (Transaction Publishers, New Brunswick: 1996).

Lansing, Robert, *The Big Four and Others of the Peace Conference* (Houghton Mifflin Company, Boston: 1921).

Lapidus, Ira M, *A History of Islamic Societies* (Cambridge University Press, Cambridge: 2002).

Laverty Miller, Joyce, 'The Syrian Revolt of 1925', *International Journal of Middle East Studies*, Vol 8, No 4 (Oct 1977) pp 545–63.

Lawrence, T E, *Seven Pillars of Wisdom* (Wordsworth, London: 1997).

Lesch, David W, *The Middle East and the United States: A Historical and Political Reassessment* (Westview Press, Boulder, Colo: 1996).

Lieshout, R H, '"Keeping Better Educated Moslems Busy": Sir Reginald Wingate and the Origins of the Husayn-McMahon Correspondence', *The Historical Journal*, Vol 27, No 2 (Jun 1984) pp 453–63.

Lloyd George, David, *The Truth About the Peace Treaties* (V Gollancz, London: 1938).

Longrigg, Stephen H, and Frank Stoakes, *Iraq* (Praeger, New York: 1959).

Louis, William Roger, *Ends of British Imperialism: The Scramble for Empire, Suez and Decolonization: Collected Essays* (I.B. Tauris, London: 2006).

Lukitz, Liora, 'The Antonius papers and the Arab awakening, over fifty years on', *Middle Eastern Studies* 30:4 (1994) pp 883–95.

MacMillan, Margaret, *Peacemakers: The Paris Peace Conference of 1919 and Its Attempt to End War* (Murray, London: 2003).

McNamara, Robert, *Britain, Nasser and the Balance of Power in the Middle East: 1952–1967: from the Egyptian Revolution to the Six-Day War* (Cass, Portland, OR: 2003).

Mansfield, Peter, and Nicolas Pelham, *A History of the Middle East* (Penguin Books, New York: 2004).

Marr, Phebe, *The Modern History of Iraq* (Westview Press, Boulder, Colo: 2004).

Mejcher, Helmut, 'British Middle East Policy 1917–21: The Inter-Departmental Level', *Journal of Contemporary History*, Vol 8, No 4 (Oct 1973) pp 81–101

Monroe, Elizabeth, *Britain's Moment in the Middle East 1914–1956* (Methuen, London: 1963).

Morris, James, *The Hashemite Kings* (Faber and Faber, London: 1959).

Nevakivi, Jukka, *Britain, France and the Arab Middle East 1914–1920* (Athlone Press, London: 1969).

Nevo, J, 'Abdullah's memoirs as historical source material' in Susser, Asher, and Aryeh Shmuelevitz (eds), *The Hashemites in the Modern Arab World: Essays in Honour of the Late Professor Uriel Dann* (Frank Cass, London: 1995).

Nicholson, James, 'The Hejaz railway', *Asian Affairs* 37:3 (2006) pp 320–36.

Ochsenwald, William, *Religion, Society, and the State in Arabia: The Hijaz Under Ottoman Control, 1840–1908* (Ohio State University Press, Columbus: 1984).

——, 'Ironic origins: Arab nationalism in the Hijaz', in Rashid Khalidi, *et al*, *The Origins of Arab Nationalism* (Columbia University Press, New York: 1991).

Paris, Timothy J, 'British Middle East Policy-Making after the First World War: The Lawrentian and Wilsonian

Schools', *The Historical Journal*, Vol 41, No 3 (Sep 1998) pp 773–93.

——, *Britain, the Hashemites, and Arab Rule, 1920–1925: The Sherifian Solution* (Frank Cass, London: 2003).

Polk, W R, and R L Chambers (eds), *Beginnings of Modernisation in the Middle East; The Nineteenth Century* (University of Chicago Press, Chicago: 1968).

Roskill, S W, *Hankey, Man of Secrets. Vol.2, 1919–1931* (Collins, London: 1972).

Rothwell, V H, 'Mesopotamia in British War Aims, 1914–1918', *The Historical Journal*, Vol 13, No 2 (Jun 1970) pp 273–94.

Russell, Malcolm B, *The First Modern Arab State: Syria Under Faysal, 1918–1920.* Studies in Middle Eastern history, no. 7 (Bibliotheca Islamica, Minneapolis: 1985).

Sachar, Howard Morley, *The Emergence of the Middle East, 1914–1924* (Allen Lane, The Penguin Press, London: 1970).

Salibi, Kamal S, *The Modern History of Jordan* (I.B. Tauris, London: 1993).

Sanders, Ronald, *The High Walls of Jerusalem: A History of the Balfour Declaration and the Birth of the British Mandate for Palestine* (Holt, Rinehart and Winston, New York: 1984).

Seale, Patrick, *The Struggle for Syria: A Study of Post-War Arab Politics, 1945–1958* (Oxford University Press, Oxford: 1965).

—— and Maureen McConville, *Assad of Syria: The Struggle for the Middle East* (University of California Press, Berkeley: 1989).

Shlaim, Avi, *Collusion Across the Jordan: King Abdullah, the Zionist Movement, and the Partition of Palestine* (Columbia University Press, New York: 1988).

——, *The Iron Wall: Israel and the Arab World* (Penguin, London: 2001).

Sharp, Alan. *The Versailles Settlement: Peacemaking in Paris, 1919.* The Making of the 20th century (St. Martin's Press, New York: 1991).

Sluggett, Peter, *Britain in Iraq: Contriving King and Country* 2nd ed (I.B. Tauris, London: 2007).

Smith, Charles D, 'The Invention of a Tradition: The Question of Arab Acceptance of the Zionist Right to Palestine during World War I', *Journal of Palestine Studies* XXII, 2 (Winter 1993) pp 48–61.

Stein, Leonard, *The Balfour Declaration* (Simon and Schuster, New York: 1961).

Storrs, Ronald, *Orientations* (I. Nicholson & Watson, London: 1939).

Strachan, Hew, *The First World War.* Vol.1, *To Arms* (Oxford University Press, Oxford: 2001).

Susser, Asher, and Aryeh Shmuelevitz (eds), *The Hashemites in the Modern Arab World: Essays in Honour of the Late Professor Uriel Dann* (Frank Cass, London: 1995).

Tanenbaum, Jan Karl, 'France and the Arab Middle East, 1914–1920', *Transactions of the American Philosophical Society,* New Ser Vol 68, No 7 (1978) pp 1–50.

Tauber, Eliezer, *The Emergence of the Arab Movements* (Frank Cass, London: 1993).

——, *The Formation of Modern Syria and Iraq* (Frank Cass, London: 1995).

Teitelbaum, Joshua, 'Sherif Hussein ibn Ali and the Hashemite vision of the post-Ottoman order: from chieftaincy to suzerainty', *Middle Eastern Studies* 34:1 (1998) pp 103–22.

——, *The Rise and Fall of the Hashimite Kingdom of Arabia* (Hurst, London: 2001).

Temperley, Harold William Vazeille (ed), *A History of the Peace Conference of Paris* Vol 6 (Frowde [u.a.], London: 1924).

Thomas, Martin, 'The Syrian Revolt and Anglo-French imperial relations, 1925–27', in Kennedy, Greg, and Keith Neilson (eds), *Incidents and International Relations: People, Power, and Personalities* (Praeger, Westport, Conn: 2002).

Tripp, Charles, *A History of Iraq* (Cambridge University Press, Cambridge: 2001).

Trumpener, Ulrich, *Germany and the Ottoman Empire, 1914–1918* (Princeton University Press, Princeton, N.J.: 1968).

Vereti, Mayir, 'The Balfour Declaration and its Makers', *Middle Eastern Studies* 6:1 (1970) pp 48–76

Vital, David, *Zionism: The Crucial Phase* (Clarendon Press, Oxford: 1987).

Westrate, Bruce, *The Arab Bureau: British Policy in the Middle East, 1916–1920* (Pennsylvania State University Press, University Park, Pa: 1992).

Wilson, Jeremy, *Lawrence of Arabia: The Authorised Biography of T.E. Lawrence* (Heinemann, London: 1989).

Wilson, Mary C, *King Abdullah, Britain, and the Making of Jordan*. Cambridge Middle East Library (Cambridge University Press, Cambridge: 1987).

Yapp, Malcolm, *The Making of the Modern Near East,
1792–1923*. A History of the Near East (Longman,
Harlow: 1987).

——, *The Near East Since the First World War: A History
to 1995*. A History of the Near East (Longman, Harlow:
1996).

Zamir, Meir, 'Faisal and the Lebanese Question, 1918–20',
Middle Eastern Studies, 27:3 (Jul 1991) pp 404–26.

Zeine, Zeine N, *The Emergence of Arab Nationalism, with
a Background Study of Arab-Turkish Relations in the
Near East* (Khayats, Beirut: 1958).

——, *The Struggle for Arab Independence; Western
Diplomacy & the Rise and Fall of Faisal's Kingdom in
Syria* (Khayats, Beirut: 1960).

Picture Sources

The author and publishers wish to express their thanks to the following sources of illustrative material and/or permission to reproduce it. They will make proper acknowledgements in future editions in the event that any omissions have occurred.

Corbis: pp 6 and 82. Getty Images: p 124.

Endpapers
The Signing of Peace in the Hall of Mirrors, Versailles, 28th June 1919 by Sir William Orpen (Imperial War Museum: Bridgeman Art Library)
Front row: Dr Johannes Bell (Germany) signing with Herr Hermann Müller leaning over him
Middle row (seated, left to right): General Tasker H Bliss, Col E M House, Mr Henry White, Mr Robert Lansing, President Woodrow Wilson (United States); M Georges Clemenceau (France); Mr David Lloyd George, Mr Andrew Bonar Law, Mr Arthur J Balfour, Viscount Milner, Mr G N Barnes (Great Britain); Prince Saionji (Japan)
Back row (left to right): M Eleftherios Venizelos (Greece);

Dr Afonso Costa (Portugal); Lord Riddell (British Press); Sir George E Foster (Canada); M Nikola Pašić (Serbia); M Stephen Pichon (France); Col Sir Maurice Hankey, Mr Edwin S Montagu (Great Britain); the Maharajah of Bikaner (India); Signor Vittorio Emanuele Orlando (Italy); M Paul Hymans (Belgium); General Louis Botha (South Africa); Mr W M Hughes (Australia)

Jacket images

(Front): Imperial War Museum: akg Images.
(Back): *Peace Conference at the Quai d'Orsay* by Sir William Orpen (Imperial War Museum: akg Images).
Left to right (seated): Signor Orlando (Italy); Mr Robert Lansing, President Woodrow Wilson (United States); M Georges Clemenceau (France); Mr David Lloyd George, Mr Andrew Bonar Law, Mr Arthur J Balfour (Great Britain); Left to right (standing): M Paul Hymans (Belgium); Mr Eleftherios Venizelos (Greece); The Emir Feisal (The Hashemite Kingdom); Mr W F Massey (New Zealand); General Jan Smuts (South Africa); Col E M House (United States); General Louis Botha (South Africa); Prince Saionji (Japan); Mr W M Hughes (Australia); Sir Robert Borden (Canada); Mr G N Barnes (Great Britain); M Ignacy Paderewski (Poland)

Index

Makers
of the
Modern
World

UK PUBLICATION: November 2008 to December 2010
CLASSIFICATION: Biography/History/
   International Relations
FORMAT: 198 × 128mm
EXTENT: 208pp
ILLUSTRATIONS: 6 photographs plus 4 maps
TERRITORY: world

Chronology of life in context, full index, bibliography innovative layout
with sidebars

Woodrow Wilson: United States of America by Brian Morton
Friedrich Ebert: Germany by Harry Harmer
Georges Clemenceau: France by David Watson
David Lloyd George: Great Britain by Alan Sharp
Prince Saionji: Japan by Jonathan Clements
Wellington Koo: China by Jonathan Clements
Eleftherios Venizelos: Greece by Andrew Dalby
From the Sultan to Atatürk: Turkey by Andrew Mango
The Hashemites: The Dream of Arabia by Robert McNamara
Chaim Weizmann: The Dream of Zion by Tom Fraser
Piip, Meierovics & Voldemaras: Estonia, Latvia & Lithuania by Charlotte Alston
Ignacy Paderewski: Poland by Anita Prazmowska
Beneš, Masaryk: Czechoslovakia by Peter Neville
Károlyi & Bethlen: Hungary by Bryan Cartledge
Karl Renner: Austria by Jamie Bulloch
Vittorio Orlando: Italy by Spencer Di Scala
Pašić & Trumbić: The Kingdom of Serbs, Croats and Slovenes by Dejan Djokic
Aleksandŭr Stamboliĭski: Bulgaria by R J Crampton
Ion Bratianu: Romania by Keith Hitchin
Paul Hymans: Belgium by Sally Marks
General Smuts: South Africa by Antony Lentin
William Hughes: Australia by Carl Bridge
William Massey: New Zealand by James Watson
Sir Robert Borden: Canada by Martin Thornton
Maharajah of Bikaner: India by Hugh Purcell
Afonso Costa: Portugal by Filipe Ribeiro de Meneses
Epitácio Pessoa: Brazil by Michael Streeter
South America by Michael Streeter
Central America by Michael Streeter
South East Asia by Andrew Dalby
The League of Nations by Ruth Henig
Consequences of Peace: The Versailles Settlement – Aftermath and Legacy
   by Alan Sharp